The Collinwood Tragedy

IN
MEMORY OF
THE UNIDENTIFIED
······DEAD······
COLLINWOOD
SCHOOL
FIRE
MAR. 4 - 1908

— SATTERFIELD —

THE
COLLINWOOD
TRAGEDY

The Story of the Worst School Fire
in American History

JAMES JESSEN BADAL

The Kent State University Press

KENT, OHIO

Frontispiece: A sentimental contemporary cartoon by Bob Satterfield emphasizing the youth and innocence of those killed in the fire. (Marshall Everett, *Complete Story of the Collinwood School Disaster and How Such Horrors Can Be Prevented* [Cleveland: N. G. Hamilton, 1908])

ISBN 978-1-60635-391-2
Manufactured in the United States of America

Cataloging information for this title is available at the Library of Congress.

24 23 22 21 20   5 4 3 2 1

To the Collinwood Nottingham Historical Society

for cooperation, trust, and patience.

The sight I witnessed in the hallway was terrible.
I cannot begin to describe it.

—Sixth-grade teacher and school principal Anna R.
Moran at the school board inquiry, March 4, 1908

I doubt if any fire department in the world could
have done any kind of effective work.

—Collinwood school superintendent Frank P. Whitney
at the coroner's inquest, March 6, 1908

CONTENTS

FOREWORD

from the Collinwood Nottingham Historical Society

"Research" is not something many of us look forward to. Before the internet, research involved long hours, in probably dusty libraries, slogging through book after book and taking notes by hand. With the coming of the internet, though, the only difference is where one sits; research still involves the same long hours, slogging through website after website, taking notes we hope we'll be able to read later—all in the name of chasing down the great stories from our past. Add to this regular trips to local cemeteries (yes, we think this is fun), exploring all those small local museums, and then finding a place to sit and try putting all this together—hoping to someday share our passion with people like you, dear Reader. And here we are, fulfilling that hope thanks to James Jessen Badal and the Kent State University Press.

We are the Collinwood Nottingham Historical Society—a small group of history buffs dedicated to remembering the history of our Collinwood community. We began as the Collinwood School Fire Centennial Commemoration Committee, formed to honor the hundredth anniversary of the Collinwood School Fire in 2008. We found, however, that we were not finished—with not only the fire's history but our community's history. We regrouped, renamed ourselves the Collinwood Nottingham Historical Society, and have been working to record and remember our history ever since.

In late 2016, we had all this marvelous research, with all kinds of new information about the fire, but nowhere to go with it. We'd done some exhibits and talks, but our real hope was, indeed, to "someday do a book." The story deserved telling; we simply didn't know how to go about doing that. Enter James Badal! In early December 2016, when we first received his email about his writing a book, we were flattered, excited, and just a tad uncertain: were we up for this? Meetings assured us he would write the story as it deserved—with the sensitivity and respect for not only the story of the fire but of the community so deeply affected by it. We already had all this information, and James Badal had the resources to expand on what we had. So the great undertaking commenced.

Thus began a couple years of questions from Badal and answers from us. Sometimes there were madcap side trips around the internet that unearthed another small fact or detail from some until-then unexplored source. And there were questions from us to him. What do you need? Did you see this? How does this fit in?

As of this writing, in late 2018, we are beginning to see the final days of this project approach. That the Collinwood Nottingham Historical Society has learned so much from this partnership goes without saying; that the Collinwood School Fire story—and our community's story—will be told in the best way possible is not in doubt.

Words are not enough to express our appreciation and thanks to James Badal and the Kent State University Press. May you, Gentle Reader, come away from this book understanding something of the resilience of our Collinwood community when tragedy struck over 110 years ago, a resilience that prevails today.

PREFACE

"But there is no villain here! How can an author *Cleveland Magazine* dubbed 'The Scholar of Evil' write a book that has no villain?" So goes the question that I was asked repeatedly as I worked on this book. And, of course, it's true: there is no villain in this terrible catastrophe—no murderous phantom lurking in the darkness, no deranged killer slicing up the bodies of his victims, no sexual deviant threatening the safety of local children. The only villain here remains the chance convergence of a number of seemingly unrelated factors that resulted in a veritable perfect storm—one of Cleveland's major disasters and the worst school fire in American history. There is also no abiding mystery as to the fire's origins, no murky secret that has kept commentators guessing for over a century; the rather mundane, easily understood cause of the blaze was determined fairly quickly.

The only melancholy mysteries associated with the catastrophe rest with the fact that nineteen of the victims were unidentified at the time and remain so today—and it has taken more than a century to arrive at an accurate list of those who died. In Cleveland, the story of the Collinwood disaster has the resonance of legend, but it remains a legend remarkably free of specific detail. A mention of the Collinwood School Fire to a contemporary Clevelander usually provokes only two responses: the death toll was high, but just how high remains unknown; and there was a mystery of some sort surrounding the doors of the building, though the exact nature of that mystery and what it may have had to do with the disaster has been long forgotten.

. . .

Although there are currently many internet sources devoted to the tragedy, the list of books dealing with the fire, either whole or in part, is not extensive. The only book written at the time of the disaster is Marshall Everett's *Complete Story of the Collinwood School Disaster and How Such Horrors Can Be Prevented*. Everett was the penname of Henry Neil (1863–1939), who sometimes went by the moniker "Judge Henry Neil." Dubbed "The Great Descriptive Writer and Historian," he authored an astonishing number of books, most dealing with catastrophic disasters and all sporting incredibly long titles. *Tragic Story of America's Greatest Disaster: Tornado, Flood and Fire in Ohio, Indiana, Nebraska and Mississippi Valley* and *Exciting Experiences in Our Wars with Spain and the Filipinos* appear in his catalog, along with books on other major catastrophes, including the sinking of the *Titanic*. He is reputed to have enjoyed relationships with American movie pioneer D. W. Griffith and the great Irish playwright George Bernard Shaw. He was also a man of strong social and political opinions, and he harbored no qualms about sharing them. Statements such as "Hoover fed the starving children in Europe and the Far East because our international bankers made big profits out of it" and "Charity pretends to feed our poor children. Charity takes 75 percent of its collections for salaries and expenses" guaranteed him publicity and a ready audience for his never-ending stream of books.

Unfortunately, there are serious issues with Everett's book on the Collinwood disaster. Poorly organized and extremely repetitious, his treatment is hobbled by all sorts of factual errors because he culled his information from a variety of different sources and paid little or no attention to the contradictions such a procedure occasionally caused. For example, over the few days following the catastrophe, Fritz Hirter, the custodian responsible for the school's two furnaces, made conflicting statements about the events leading up to the fire. Everett quotes all of his statements but makes no attempt to resolve the inconsistencies among them. Sometimes something as simple and easily corrected as the misspelling of a name goes unnoticed. Everett fills his book with extensive quotations from those directly involved in the incident, but he does not specify his sources—the investigation convened by the Collinwood Board of Education on the day of the fire and the official inquest of Cuyahoga County's coroner, Thomas Burke, which began on March 5 and lasted for six days, or one of Cleveland's daily papers.

Most modern readers also would find the exaggerated sentimentality of his writing style unbearably heavy-handed and more appropriate for a cheap romance novel. The over-the-top opening of the publisher's preface prepares the reader for the emotional wallowing to come: "Amid sobs and groans, from white, trembling lips comes the story of the fearful disaster at North Collinwood, Ohio, where 172 children and two heroic women teachers went down to death in the ruins of the schoolhouse, which was swept by flames." "The story, sad and thrilling in the extreme," Everett writes in the author's preface, "will deal with the vain fight made by the victims . . . of the desperate efforts of heroic men and women to snatch from the jaws of death their own loved ones."

The stories he tells are, indeed, heart-wrenching in the extreme; and while one wants to trust his accounts, his refusal to identify sources and his false claim that he was present as the disaster unfolded—no doubt made to add a note of authenticity—call into question the veracity of at least some of his narrative. "Standing beside the red-hot embers of the schoolhouse and watching weeping men draw from the ruins shapeless masses that were once laughing, happy boys and girls, I witnessed a scene so terrible that my pen almost refuses to write the sickening story of the disaster that brought grief to every family in the little village, and which depopulated the town of young people." It is also interesting to note that the word *little* would seem Everett's favorite adjective: "little children" (The oldest pupils at the school were fifteen!), "little bones," "little bodies," "their little songs," "their little prayers." This constant sentimentalizing does a distinct disservice to history and memories of the victims. Not all the pupils at the school were picture-perfect children. Lakeview Elementary School had its share of street kids, and the janitor occasionally caught some of the older boys smoking in the basement.

Thus, to appreciate and understand fully the true depths of the catastrophe in Collinwood, it is necessary to separate the event from the often hysterical language Everett employed to describe it. He constantly records the anguished outcries of grieving parents and siblings in the victims' homes, but it is simply impossible to accept that Everett was actually present at so many different locations at precisely the right moment to catch these painful outbursts. Granted, Everett never claimed that his book was a scholarly treatise, and since it was written in the shadow of the tragedy, it cannot be dismissed outright. It remains, however, a period curio—a pulp treatment of a terrible and significant historical incident.

In more recent times, the story of the Collinwood catastrophe has appeared as a single chapter in large anthologies devoted to all sorts of disasters, such as Troy Taylor and Rene Kruse's *And Hell Followed with It* (2010) and John Stark Bellamy's *Cleveland's Greatest Disasters* (2009). The only modern book-length treatment of the fire is Edward Kern's *The Collinwood School Fire of 1908* (1993). Kern's work is solid, serious, and very detailed. It also benefits enormously from the author's obvious devotion to his subject. For him, the story is profoundly personal; he lost four of his forbears in the tragedy. Working in the later years of the twentieth century, he also enjoyed access to a number of people involved, who have since passed on. Unfortunately, as it is a self-published book, Kern's volume is not widely available outside of Cleveland.

In 1908, Cleveland boasted four major daily papers: the *Plain Dealer, Press, Leader,* and *News.* Their coverage of the disaster is the only other readily available and reasonably reliable source of information. Although the leading papers of other major cities published extensive articles dealing with the catastrophe—the story's horrific nature guaranteed coverage all over the country (Newspapers.com lists 27,055 articles on the disaster in the nation's newspapers, 14,272 in Ohio alone)—the Cleveland dailies remain virtually the only available sources of information actually gathered on-site as the tragedy unfolded. Newspapers, however, come with their own problems. In the early years of the twentieth century, the spirit of no-holds-barred yellow journalism—born out of the New York circulation wars between Joseph Pulitzer and William Randolph Hearst—was still riding high in the American press. The Cleveland dailies provided readers with headlines and stories as wildly sensational as anything to be found in Marshall Everett's book. In its March 4 evening edition, the *Press* proclaimed, "North Collinwood School Destroyed and Little Ones, Caught Like Rats in Trap, Die in Flames." On March 5, the *News* described the scene at the makeshift morgue in exceptionally gruesome and sickening detail: "Row on row of charred corpses, headless torsos with blackened flesh, half naked bodies with splintered bones protruding, crumbling stubs of hands crossed before unrecognizable faces." The accounts of the disaster in all of the contemporary sources suffer from sensationalism in varying degrees. None of the details surrounding this catastrophe need embellishment to make them more compelling; all of the elements of the Collinwood School Fire story are already sufficiently compelling and heartbreaking—indeed, beyond imagination. The sights, sounds, and smells that assaulted and overwhelmed would-be rescuers and onlookers on that terrible morning! The panic and suffering experienced by those in the burning building! The ordeals parents endured as they watched fire destroy the school and tried desperately to identify the bodies of their children at the makeshift morgue!

My good friend the late Doris O'Donnell Beaufait, former dean of female newspaper reporters in Cleveland, once described a newspaper story as "history in a hurry"—a transitory account to be digested quickly, discarded, and replaced the next day. Unfortunately, in the drive to get that history on the streets as fast as possible, especially in a city boasting more than one daily paper, inaccuracies, gloss-overs, half-truths, and misconceptions of various kinds often creep into the coverage. A reporter on the scene, trying to accurately record the details of a rapidly unfolding disaster such as the Collinwood School Fire, is limited to what he can see and hear. No one is going to be able to answer a newspaperman's questions thoughtfully when he or she is swept up in utter chaos. Journalistic principles were also nowhere near as rigorous in the early twentieth century as they are today. Modern standards, for example, mandate that in cases of attribution, a reporter or writer provide an individual's full name and title, if relevant. Unfortunately for a modern-day researcher, those standards did not prevail in the early years of the twentieth century; editors and reporters apparently deemed full names unimportant. Although initials sometimes appear, the significant figures in contemporary newspaper accounts of the fire are usually stripped of their first names and appear simply as "Fire Marshal Brockman" or "Mayor Westropp." Newspapers also rarely followed up on details of a story. An investigative initiative may be announced on a given day, but there will be nothing in print reporting the results of that initiative unless it proves newsworthy. A researcher will also occasionally encounter moments of genuine though unintended hilarity because no one apparently paid any attention to the effect created during the layout process of juxtaposing two articles of radically different character on the same page. In one such instance, a serious article about the fire appears alongside one bearing the title "How She Got Rid of Her Fat."

There are also some inherent problems with the quotations that appear in all four major Cleveland papers. Reporters obviously targeted anyone involved in the tragedy directly or indirectly: students who escaped, parents of both the living and the dead, teachers, onlookers, police, firemen, would-be rescuers, and officials representing Collinwood, Cleveland, and the Collinwood schools. Their printed statements, which reporters had supposedly taken on-site, often read as if the speaker had carefully considered them—not quite what one would expect from someone living through and trying to process such a horrendous occurrence!

The veracity of the printed statements is not at issue, but the recorded language in which the statement is made occasionally is. Have any of these utterances been regularized or cleaned up—especially if the source is a nonnative speaker—by either the writer of the story or an editor, and, if so, to what degree? It is also sometimes difficult to ascertain where and under what circumstances a quoted individual made that statement attributed to him or her: on the scene of the tragedy, at the speaker's home, at a largely impromptu investigative meeting of Collinwood officialdom, or at the coroner's official inquest? The copies of the coroner's original subpoenas ordering witnesses to appear at the formal inquest, on file at the medical examiner's office, make it clear whom he called to testify at the proceedings and on which day that individual was to appear. By comparing the date of the individual's appearance with the date of the newspaper story, one can get a reasonably good idea of whether a given statement was made at the inquest.

The *Press* ran brief stories allegedly written by people directly involved in the incident—specifically the Cleveland fire department's chief George A. Wallace, third-grade teacher Lulu Rowley, and Coroner Burke. (The paper continued this practice at least into the 1930s.) Did the alleged writer of record actually pen the short piece that bears his or her name, or was it written by a staff reporter? If the individual whose name appears with the story wrote it, to what degree had it been cleaned up or altered by a second party? Or is it possible that an anonymous staffer actually composed the piece based on an extended interview, and the interviewee merely allowed his or her name to be attached to it? Such niceties may not matter significantly with "history in a hurry," but they assume enormous importance and significance when the goal is to construct an accurate historical record.

. . .

Historical incidents remain a collection of the verifiable facts and utterances that make that event significant, but the mundane details of day-to-day life that run concurrently with that occurrence are rarely remembered, precisely because they seem so ordinary. An elderly gentleman contacted me over twenty years ago, while I was working on the first edition of *In the Wake of the Butcher*. Not only had he been present when police discovered the second set of Flo Polilo's remains, he had delivered newspapers in the shantytowns! From him, I learned that a number of the residents that lived in that squalor did have jobs—and could, therefore, afford a daily paper—but didn't earn enough to live anywhere else. He also recounted that the smell of cooking chickens seemed to hang perpetually over the camps. Chicken dealers would come to town twice a week and set up stands along Carnegie Avenue. They would throw the birds that hadn't survived the trip in the alleys off the street where they were collected and cooked by residents in the hobo jungles. Similarly, the Collinwood tragedy unfolded against a background of mundane details that characterized ordinary day-to-day life in that place, at that time: a rapidly developing village in the early years of the twentieth century where the streets were not paved and a group of volunteers made up the fire department; a town where a large immigrant population that spoke little or no English tried to a make a life for itself in the new world alongside neighbors who could trace their ancestry back to the original settlers of the Western Reserve.

. . .

Like any historical event of primarily local significance, the account of the Collinwood School Fire comes down to the present age as a set of pieces from an incomplete puzzle: snapshots of chaos and fragments of stories captured in newspaper accounts, official documents, and simple rumors that have been passed along and embellished for decades. The tale of the disaster is also about far more than the fire and the resulting loss of life. The catastrophe generated a number of related stories, all of which move forward simultaneously—rather like the separate instrumental lines in a full orchestra score.

The complex series of plot lines began when Emma Neibert first noticed the wisps of smoke rising out of cracks in the first-floor stairs, a discovery that led to a panicked stampede inside the school—the utter chaos of nine teachers trying to control and then save the pupils in overcrowded classrooms. Outside the building, desperate parents and would-be rescuers fought almost impossible odds to save as many children as possible while Collinwood's wholly inadequate volunteer fire department—joined by members of the Cleveland fire department—fought a losing battle with the rapidly spreading blaze. Police had to be called to control the crowd gathering around the burning school, which included curious onlookers as well as horrified neighborhood residents and hysterical parents.

Toward the end of the day, the almost unimaginable scenes at the makeshift morgue, where parents sought to identify their children among the badly burned corpses, unfolded against a backdrop of official inquiries generated by the disaster: the Collinwood Board of Education, the Cuyahoga County Coroner's Office, and various building inspectors representing local and state agencies. Official and unofficial statements about the fire and the conditions that led to it from a variety of sources played out against days of solemn funerals and pronouncements of aid, financial and otherwise, to bereaved parents and the shattered neighborhood. All of these story lines ultimately came together in a series of recommendations concerning the design not just of schools but of all public buildings.

. . .

The emotional depths of the tragedy in Collinwood lie beyond comprehension: a village with a population of only about 8,000 lost 172 of its school-age children in just a few hours on an early March morning in 1908. Indeed, some families lost all their children in the catastrophe. Over the years, there have been vague though persistent rumors that some deeply traumatized families summarily moved out of the neighborhood, leaving everything behind, including their bank accounts. The story of the Collinwood School Fire remains far more than simply an account of one terrible day in the life of an industrial turn-of-the-century village in northeastern Ohio.

It is the tale of local officialdom that rose to the occasion and reached out to immigrant families unsure of their rights at a time when their lives were shattered. It is an account of city charities, churches, and relief agencies responding immediately to an unimaginable disaster with medical help, comfort for the bereaved, and financial support for those who could not afford the trappings of a proper funeral. It is the story of local fundraising efforts that netted $50,000, more than $1 million today, to provide food, coal, and other necessities for the poor families of the neighborhood. It is a series of stories about local businesses and individuals that donated everything from money to formal clothes to wear at the seemingly unending procession of solemn funerals. Finally, it is the story of a resilient community that survived a catastrophe virtually beyond imagination.

NOTE

The biographical details concerning Marshall Everett can be found on the Iroquois Theater website, while his daunting list of books is published on John Mark Ockerbloom's Online Books Page.

ACKNOWLEDGMENTS

I am indebted to a number of organizations that provided valuable assistance during the research and writing of this book. First, I thank Cuyahoga Community College for granting me the second full-year sabbatical that I have enjoyed in my long tenure at the institution.

I owe a major debt of gratitude to the Collinwood Nottingham Historical Society—principally Mary Louise Jesek Daley and Elva Brodnick, for constant support and patience. Since the hundredth anniversary of the Collinwood School Fire in 2008, the society has been on an intense scavenger hunt for anything related to the neighborhood disaster, any stray bit of information, any small, hitherto unrecognized piece of the vast puzzle. The amount of material the society has unearthed is incredible. Its members have gathered enough photographs and other pieces of illustration to fill a coffee-table book, enough pieces of information and stray bits of color related to the tragedy to warrant an encyclopedia. Would that we could have included it all!

On the hundredth anniversary of the Collinwood School Fire, the Cleveland Public Library assembled the significant documents related to the event and prepared a tribute to those who lost their lives. I am indebted to library staff for giving me access to this important material and for patiently guiding me through the intricacies of scanning and copying in the digital age.

Thanks also to staff members at Lake View Cemetery for searching through old records related to the burial of the nineteen unidentified victims and others killed in the catastrophe.

Finally, a thank-you to Hugh Shannon at the Cuyahoga County Medical Examiner's Office for scrolling through miles of microfilm in search of some of the original documentation associated with the tragedy.

Chapter One

"CRIES AND WHISPERS"

Lake View Cemetery, on Cleveland's East Side, ranks as one of the city's most famous landmarks, a crown jewel bordered by East Cleveland, Cleveland Heights, and Little Italy. The site is dominated by the James A. Garfield Monument, the final resting place of the country's twentieth president and his wife, a towering structure that not only provides visitors with an impressive view of the city skyline but also looks out over a maze of winding roads and trails, beautiful gardens, huge old trees providing perpetual shade, imposing mausoleums, and the impressive statues and elaborate grave markers so typical of an earlier age. To drive or stroll through Lake View Cemetery's trails and byways is to thumb casually through the pages of Cleveland history; many of the most prominent names in the city's past and major figures from the Western Reserve lie buried here. In 1997, Eliot Ness's ashes were scattered over Wade Lake during a ceremony honoring the city's onetime (1935–41) safety director. Cutting though the cemetery during rush hour can sometimes be a handy way of avoiding heavy homeward-bound traffic for residents of the older outer-ring suburbs of the city's East Side.

Late one quiet afternoon about ten years ago, a good friend and colleague was driving his three-year-old daughter to their Cleveland Heights home after her lesson at the Music School Settlement. Given the late afternoon hour, he opted for the Lake View Cemetery detour. Besides, his daughter always enjoyed visiting President Garfield. On

I

this particular day, she gazed casually out the passenger window of the family car as her father drove slowly over the narrow cemetery roads toward the Mayfield Road entrance and their Cleveland Heights home. "You should go down this way, Daddy," she remarked suddenly, indicating the direction she wished him to take. Without comment, he turned the car down the route she had designated.

The narrow, winding road led to the lower end of the sprawling cemetery grounds, close to the Euclid Avenue entrance. They passed the huge grave markers and the heavily weathered statues of angels—heads bowed, arms raised, wings arched. As they approached the northwest edge of section 25, a simple monument of gray stone standing close to the road came into view. At the midway point on one side, a weathered bronze plaque depicted a grieving angel with outstretched wings sheltering half a dozen clearly distressed children; on the reverse side, a similarly aged plaque bore an alarmingly long list of names. To the left of the monument rested an old headstone inscribed with "Grace M. Fiske—Sister" as well as a quote from the Book of Isaiah: "He will swallow up death in victory." To the right stood a similar marker, inscribed "Leonard"—below which three names were listed: Herbert, Arline, and Louise. All three had been born in the waning years of the nineteenth century; all three had met untimely deaths in 1908. In the late afternoon stillness, the air of solemnity was palpable. The young girl gazed out the passenger-side window as if listening to a whispered message that only she could hear. The questioning look on her father's face prompted a response both simple and utterly mystifying: "I have friends here."

. . .

It is obviously a very old film. Etched numbers and a multitude of scratches flicker by before the first image appears. Initially, it isn't even clear what one is seeing. The picture is so indistinct and murky; it would seem to be a picture of a ruin of some sort. As the camera pans slowly to the left, a huge, encrusted object resembling an old ship's anchor embedded at the bottom of the sea appears. Suddenly, the ghostly figure of a man seems to rise almost out of nothing and then just as quickly disappears. The film abruptly cuts to a large Romanesque arch; at the bottom, several shadowy figures seem to mill about aimlessly. There are some buildings visible behind them, but, largely because of the blurry quality of the images, it's impossible to tell whether they are houses or storefronts. When the camera pans slowly back to the left, a small patch of dying flames appears. Suddenly, all becomes clear; the picture is cloudy at least partly because of smoke. One is seeing smoldering ruins. It's a very short piece of film, a mere fifty-three seconds of catastrophe's aftermath.

. . .

March 4, 2017, the intersection of East 152nd Street and Lucknow Avenue, Collinwood. The winds from Canada coming down over Lake Erie can be both a blessing and a curse for the communities like Collinwood, which grew and thrived along the lake's southern shore. During the hazy days of summer, those refreshing breezes cool the air and bring the unmistakable scent of a large body of water. Winter winds, however, often carry freezing temperatures and occasionally crippling quantities of snow. On this particular day, the weather is unremarkable: calm, upper twenties, and nary a hint of snow on the ground or in the air—remarkably similar to what it was on this same day one hundred and nine years ago.

Collinwood is one of the city's older neighborhoods. Though the forces of renewal are making major inroads in some sections, the area around this intersection appears a little worse for wear and a bit seedy. The streets are narrow, the houses old and in need of some maintenance, the small front yards a bit scraggly. It's difficult to imagine what this section of the neighborhood must have looked like over one hundred years ago. Even though East 152nd Street is a major artery that runs through some of the neighborhood's commercial areas, it is remarkably quiet, even in the middle of the day. Cars drift by slowly; local residents stroll by casually and seemingly unconcerned. How can they be so blasé? Don't they know what happened here?

There's a parking lot to the west of East 152nd—obviously belonging to the school that stands back from the street. The reasonably large parking area must encroach on the footprint of the original building that once stood here. On the northeast corner of the lot is a raised garden—perhaps three feet high—surrounded on all four sides by sloping stone walls. During the warm months of spring and summer, the garden undoubtedly flourishes; now, in the dead of winter, it appears barren and quiet. Many of the bricks are inscribed with the names of individuals and organizations, a simple memorial or a recognition of some sort of financial support. Benches face the raised area on three sides of the garden square, inviting the passerby or visitor to sit quietly and, perhaps, meditate on the event the garden memorializes.

It is said that a heavy atmosphere of dread and gloom invariably hovers over plots of ground, such as old battlefields, where multiple deaths have occurred; the acutely sensitive can sometimes discern the

The memorial plaque at Lake View Cemetery. Photo by Mark Wade Stone. (Courtesy StoryWorks.TV)

distant yet palpable echo of the carnage. If there are restless spirits anywhere in Cleveland, surely they would be here. Those claiming to possess a touch of psychic awareness have reported hearing faint cries, feeling small hands grabbing at their clothes, or being assailed suddenly by an odor so terrible and foul that it drives them away. On the east side of the garden facing East 152nd, a shrub-lined path leads from the sidewalk to the garden and the bronze plaque on its side:

> On this site, Ash Wednesday, March 4, 1908, 172 children, 2 teachers and 1 rescuer perished in the Collinwood, Lakeview School Fire. The worst school fire this nation ever witnessed.

NOTES

The event described in the opening section harks back to a time in this young girl's life when she seemed curiously sensitive to what many would call the paranormal. Her father shared this intriguing story with the understanding that I would respect their privacy. While this girl, now a teenager, is no longer prone to these encounters with the spirit world, at the time of this incident, she was—as she still is—deathly afraid of fire. Though her first name is not particularly unusual, it is not as common today as it once was, and it is worth noting that the young woman in question shares that name with one of the identified victims of the disaster.

William Hubern Bullock made the short film described in the text. The original copy is part of the collection of the Motion Picture, Broadcast and Recorded Sound Division in the Library of Congress. It was transferred to DVD for the Cleveland Public Library in 2008, and the library has made it available on YouTube.

Chapter Two

COLLINWOOD

Pursuing the American Dream
along the Erie Shore

The Collinwood neighborhood, on Cleveland's near east side, has experienced more socioeconomic ups and downs in its long history than the roller-coaster rides at Euclid Beach Park that once stood on the area's northwest edge. In the years following World War II, Collinwood ranked among the heaviest industrial areas in the country: more than a dozen firms—including Fisher Body, General Electric, Lincoln Electric, Hamilton Steel, and Lindsay Wire—drew European immigrants and migrant workers from Virginia, Kentucky, and Tennessee to the shores of Lake Erie. But the second half of the twentieth century brought a series of social ills that resulted in declining property values and serious economic collapse. In other old inner-city Cleveland neighborhoods, such as Tremont and Ohio City, the forces of renewal and regeneration have already waged successful battles against years of neglect and blight. Today, in the second decade of the twenty-first century, entrepreneurs and artists with a sense of civic dedication, as well as young people in search of affordable housing and possessing healthy hunger for urban adventure, are gradually transforming a neighborhood once hobbled by a plummeting economy, property devaluation, serious racial strife, and crippling gang wars.

Originally a part of what was designated East Cleveland Township, Collinwood once bore the unlikely name of Frogsville, apparently because the surrounding swampland was an ideal breeding ground for frogs. Tracing the area's growth and its name change from a moniker that suggested a village of amphibians (with all the attendant jokes about "croaking") to the much statelier and civically appropriate *Collinwood* involves an exceedingly complex journey through the vagaries and occasional mistakes of old county public records. Early in the nineteenth century, Mrs. A. P. Burton came to the settlement to teach; in 1880, she wrote of life in the wilderness of northeast Ohio as she had first found it: "The same week the school directors came for me to teach the school in Frogville [*sic*], now Collinwood; went down in an ox team; the roads were just logs thrown together, very rough. Taught three months; stayed in Mr. Hale's family, now all dead."

Had it not been for the railroads—that massive industrial power of the nineteenth century that bound the sprawling country together and provided a driving force to its burgeoning economy—this sparsely populated settlement would most likely have remained a tiny blip on the map of Cuyahoga County. Thanks to both its geographically strategic position between major northeast cities and the fact that the land area around it was flat, Frogsville gradually became a major railroad hub. In 1848, the newly established Cleveland, Painesville & Ashtabula Railroad provided a small but important link in the route between Chicago and Buffalo. A massive railroad complex would sprout from these humble beginnings and continue to grow well into the twentieth century—bringing with it support businesses, a huge population increase in a very short time span, pollution in the form of smoke and soot, strained public services, and the social problems that often accompany rapid population growth.

In 1924, William R. Coates wrote in *A History of Cuyahoga County and the City of Cleveland,* "This township [East Cleveland], which is classed

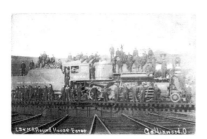

The railroad yards became Collinwood's major employer and the catalyst for the village's rapid population growth. (Courtesy of the Collinwood Nottingham Historical Society)

with the early Survey townships of the Reserve, does not appear on the early maps of Cuyahoga County and does not appear on the present maps. It has been said of it that it has had more varied municipal relations and more irregular boundaries than any other township in the county." Perhaps, nothing illustrates Coates's confusion more than the subsequent bewildering parade of name changes for the area, none of which ever made it clear as to just what part of the land mass those new monikers referred. According to records of the Cuyahoga County commissioners, the village of Collamer was established in the area that would ultimately become Collinwood on February 3, 1872—named after Judge Jacob Collamer, postmaster for the Collamer area in the 1850s. In 1874, the Lake Shore & Michigan Southern Railroad chose the area as the site for a railyard, a huge company roundhouse for the servicing of the line's locomotives, a machine shop, company offices, and apartments for company employees. In an act of homage to John Collins, the first engineer on the line, the powers that be rechristened the settlement Collinsville Station. On June 4, 1883, Collinwood Village was established from land taken from both East Cleveland and Euclid Townships, and on April 18, 1896, Collinwood Village became Collinwood Township.

The massive number of rail lines generated by all this economic activity ultimately grew into a line of demarcation that bisected the Collinwood neighborhood as effectively as the Mason-Dixon line had divided the country in the years leading up to the Civil War. The area south of the Erie shore and extending down to the railroad lines became known as either North Collinwood or Waterloo Beach, the neighborhood south of the lines, simply South Collinwood. Thanks in part to the railroads, by the 1870s the area had become the largest supplier of grapes in the entire country. By the end of World War II, the entire area had become a major hub of railroad activity for the New York Central and later for the Penn Central Transportation Company. In 1976, the entire complex would come under the control of Conrail.

Education became a top priority for the rapidly growing immigrant population. Many of the new residents came from nations where education was never universal and rarely free. The first Collinwood

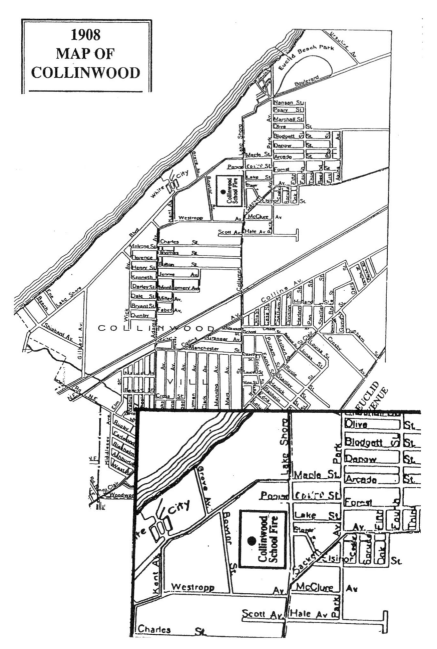

Map of Collinwood in 1908. The inset at the lower right shows areas around Lakeview Elementary School.

schoolhouse was built in 1864, and even the poorest families made the financial sacrifices necessary to provide their children with school supplies. The spiritual needs of the growing community, however, went largely unnoticed until 1867, when the First Congregational Church of Collinwood was established, to be followed two years later by the Collinwood Christian Church.

. . .

The year 1900 was approaching rapidly, bringing with it the new century's promise of fresh beginnings and renewal. The genteel and stately era of the nineteenth century came to a symbolic close in January 1901 when Queen Victoria died, and an exuberant period of twentieth-century American optimism began the same year, when Theodore Roosevelt was elected president and teddy bears became the national craze and the most preferred Christmas present. For Collinwood the future looked exceedingly bright. As an independent community, Collinwood Township had prospered to the point that it had its own local government, police force, volunteer fire department, and school system. The village had developed into a thriving melting pot; European immigrants mixed—though not always easily—with transplants from the southern states and the representatives of those august families who traced their ancestry to the Western Reserve's original settlers.

According to the 1900 US Census, the village's population stood at just under four thousand; within six years, it had nearly doubled. The driving force behind this expansion, of course, remained the railroads, as well as all the ancillary and support businesses and industries. Irish, Italian, and Slovenian immigrants were the major ethnic groups pouring into the area. The Slovenian population congregated north of the railroad lines, in the area known as North Collinwood or Waterloo Beach, and the Italians gathered in South Collinwood, south of the railroad lines. (At the time, Cleveland boasted six Italian neighborhoods of varying sizes.) Many of Collinwood's new Italian residents drifted from the ethnic enclaves on the East Side: "Big Italy" close to downtown and "Little Italy" farther east.

Most transplants sought employment with the railroads or in related industries, and many found living accommodations with already established households. Large families tended to be the rule in Collinwood; it was not unusual for there to be a nearly twenty-year age span among as many as ten children. When the older sons married and moved out, households often took in boarders to fill the vacancies and supplement the family income. A check of the 1900 census records for Collinwood shows it was not unusual to see a family of five or six renting out living space to as many as four boarders.

The neighborhood badly needed a new elementary school. The old facility, built in 1864 on the corner of Collamer and School Streets, and the newer building, on Clarke Avenue, erected in 1889, could no longer handle the steadily growing population of school-age children. Since the village was an independent municipal entity with no political connections with Cleveland, all the responsibility for planning the project, paying for it, and seeing it through to completion rested

COLLAMER STREET LOOKING NORTH COLLINWOOD, OHIO

A contemporary photograph of Collamer Street, now East 152nd Street, looking north. Lakeview Elementary School would be on the left side at the upper end of the street. (Courtesy The Cleveland *Press* Collection, Michael Schwartz Library, Cleveland State University)

The proliferation of saloons and cafés was one of the inevitable results of Collinwood's rapid population growth. Pictured here is the C. B. Lake Café at 667 Collamer. (Courtesy The Walter Leedy Postcard Collection, The Cleveland *Press* Collection, Michael Schwartz Library, Cleveland State University)

with the local school board. Sources differ as to which local architect received the board's nod, John Eisenmann or Paul C. Searles. Both men were eminently qualified and boasted impressive résumés that included some of Cleveland's major buildings. The former taught at Case School of Applied Science and had designed and overseen the construction of a large number of local landmarks, the most famous of which remains the elaborately impressive Euclid Arcade—a massive project accomplished in collaboration with George H. Smith. The later was a partner in Searles, Hirsh & Gavin, a local firm responsible for a number of structures, notably the thirteen-story Swetland Building, built in 1910 at the corner of Euclid Avenue and East Ninth Street in downtown Cleveland.

Actually, both men contributed to the finished 1907–8 building. Eisenmann had designed and completed what would become the first phase of the building that opened in 1901—two floors, each housing two classrooms and an attic initially intended for storage. When the original school building needed renovation and expansion in 1907 due to the ever increasing population of students, Eisenmann drew up the plans calling for four additional rooms, two per floor, to be added to the rear of the building; but the firm of Searles, Hirsh & Gavin even handled the construction after making some adjustments to Eisenmann's original design—a notable collaboration between two competing firms. Named the Lakeview Elementary School, the original building—facing Collamer (now East 152nd Street) between Sackett Avenue to the south and Maple Street to the north—opened in 1901 and served students from kindergarten through sixth grade.

The 1907 expanded facility was a modern building: a three-story structure with eight classrooms, four per floor, and a third floor "attic" originally intended as either an auditorium or a gymnasium. An open central area of the building contained two staircases. Two large coal-burning boilers in the basement in the middle of the building provided steam heat through a network of insulated pipes to cast-iron radiators. In one sense, the building optimized the last word in

The new Lakeview Elementary School on Collamer as it looked at the beginning of the 1907–8 academic year. Originally built in 1901 and expanded in 1907, the structure represented the last word in state-of-the-art school design and construction of the period. (Courtesy of the Collinwood Nottingham Historical Society)

modernity: there were no gas lines; electricity provided the necessary power. For some reason, all restroom facilities had been relegated to the basement; hence, any pupil on the second or third floor wishing to relieve himself or herself faced quite a journey. The janitor's closet, containing a full arsenal of cleaning supplies and other tools designed to keep the building clean and in working order, also occupied space in the basement, under the doors to the outside that faced east. The building additionally included other vital necessities for a modern schoolhouse: teachers' rooms and cloakrooms. Its exterior was stone; most of its interior—floors and stairs—Georgia pine.

Due to the nature of the Collinwood tragedy, every detail of the building's planning, construction, and renovation assumed major importance in the aftermath of the disaster. It is a significant part of the neighborhood's history. In more recent years, there have been questions as to exactly how the architect or builder added the four new classrooms to the original structure. No floor plans of the original building have so far come to light, and all existing photographs of the school, which date from the period after the additions of 1907, show a three-story building whose dimensions and proportions seem whole and complete. It is almost impossible to understand how the four rooms could have been added externally to the original building; nothing visible even remotely gives the impression of an added wing. Though it would be understandable to assume that the new rooms were created by reconfiguring the existing space, contemporary documents do state they were added on to the west end of the building. Careful examination of photographs reveal that that was, indeed, the case, and a present-day observer can only admire the skill with which architect Paul C. Searles made the addition without having it stick out like the proverbial sore thumb. The exact 1908 specifications for the building—included here—can be found in the Cleveland Inspection Bureau's "Editorial Comment and Report of the Collinwood School Disaster," issued on April 6, 1908.

The building was three stories in height, with basement and attic, outside dimension's being 66 x 84 ft. outside brick walls 12-inches-12 [*sic*] inches-12 inches thick, with substantial brick piers, and four interior 12-inch cross walls rising to the attic, gable hip slate roof, on wood sheathing; ordinary timber and joist construction, lathered and plastered; ceilings of lath and plaster mainly and part wood sheathed; floors were single ⁷∕₈-inch tongued and grooved boards, the greater part of the basement floor being cement; one interior main hall-court, with doors leading into each class room, and having stairway at east and west sides of hall leading to separate exists on each floor; iron fire escape on east side of building [the sole fire escape was actually on the north side]. Building has no outward exposure.

Though the school looks huge in contemporary photographs, its dimensions were actually rather modest. A library had been tucked in

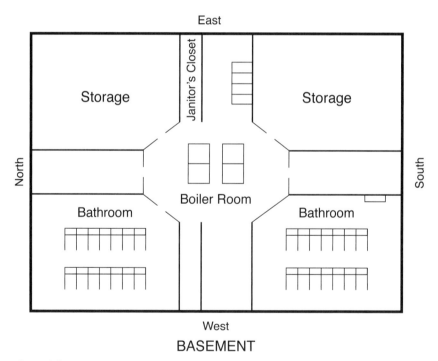

BASEMENT

This and facing page: Contemporary plans of the school's basement, first, and second floors. Note the school's single fire escape on the north side of the building (on the left side of the floorplan here). To date, no contemporary floorplan of the modified third floor has come to light.

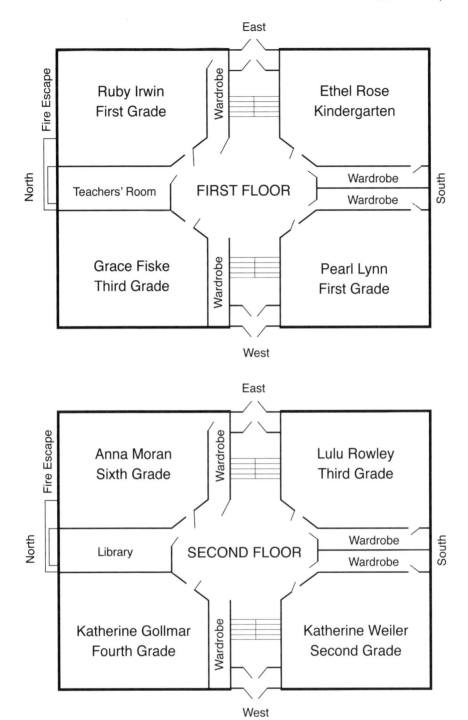

between the fourth- and sixth-grade classrooms at the north end of the second floor; but judging by surviving floor plans, the space was of only moderate size. In the disaster's immediate aftermath, the nature and placement of the two doorways leading out of the building—one facing east, the other west—would become a hot issue. There were actually four sets of double doors. At both the east and west ends, an interior set opened into a small vestibule that led to the exterior doors. Each half of the double-door system measured approximately two and a half to three feet. During off-school hours, these points of exterior entrance and exit obviously were kept securely locked. During the school day, each right-hand door fastened to the top of the door-frame with a spring lock while the left-hand door swung freely. There was a fire-alarm system, but it only alerted those in the building; there was no connection to the local volunteer fire department or any other outside facility. Fire drills were standard procedure at the school, but they only channeled pupils to the central staircases and ultimately out the two exits at the west and east ends, not to the fire escape.

By fall 1907, the student population had already outgrown the newly expanded facility. The building had to accommodate some-where between 350 and 366 pupils. It was hardly unusual for a single classroom to hold more than forty students. Whatever its original purpose, the third-floor space was commandeered into classroom service. There had been three fire drills during the fall-winter months before the fire. Reportedly, there had been one in late January or early February, approximately three weeks before the disaster. Supposedly, the entire building could be successfully evacuated in two minutes or less—a claim that would seem hard to support, considering the number of children at the school and that there were only two exits.

As the population continued to grow, so did the need for funds to provide public services. The city of Cleveland proper was absorbing—some might say gobbling up—the outlying rural areas; consequently, Collinwood began to look to the metropolis with envious eyes for its far greater financial resources. The local political discourse began to flirt with the notion of annexation to its neighbor to the west. The citizenry, indeed, voted for the proposed alliance; but the regime of then mayor Sherman engaged in a fight for its political life and marshaled the anti-annexation forces sufficiently to delay the proposed merger—at least for a while. Unfortunately, with the promise of a civic union looming, Collinwood's city council grew reluctant to spend any money on public services, such as the fire department, preferring to wait until Cleveland would absorb such costs. Notably, considering the events of 1908, the original plans for Lakeview Elementary School called for fire escapes to be installed on three sides of the building. According to the March 8, 1908, *Plain Dealer,* W. A. Stevens, the builder of the structure's single fire escape, had lobbied the school board heavily for the additional means of escape, but it resisted due to the cost. Hence, the only exterior means stood on the building's north side. It would seem cost-saving measures had become the rule for Collinwood officialdom in the months leading up to March 4, 1908.

· · ·

In the early years of the twentieth century, virtually the only professions open to women who chose not to marry early were nursing and teaching. At the beginning of the 1907–8 school year, the educational needs of those 350-plus students at the Lakeview School were being met by nine single women, all in their twenties but for sixth-grade teacher and school principal Anna Moran, who was most likely over forty. Very little information about these teachers has come down to the present, except for their names and the few details of their ordinary lives that can be gleaned from public documents that are sometimes compromised by simple misspellings and other common errors, such as mistakes regarding residence and year of birth.

Very young children would have obvious difficulty navigating staircases that reached to the third floor; and in recognition of that simple truth, the two first-grade classrooms and the kindergarten were on the first floor. Ethel A. Rose supervised the kindergarten class in the southeast corner of the building. Rose remains perhaps the most obscure of the nine teachers. According to the 1900 US Census, she was born in Ohio in 1881 and lived with her widowed mother in Independence, Ohio. In 1907, she made her home at 959 Adams Avenue in Collinwood.

The nine teachers at Lakeview Elementary School in 1908. (Courtesy collinwood fire.org)

The two first-grade classes rested in the capable hands of Ruby Irwin and Pearl P. Lynn. The former also remains elusive; the most likely candidate among every Ruby Irwin listed in public documents is Ruby Bell Irwin, who appears in both the 1911 and 1913 Cleveland City Directories as a teacher whose residence in 1913 was on Prospect. Her domain was in the northeast corner of the school. Judging by the one very poor photograph of her that has survived, she seems to have been among the eldest of group. Pearl P. Lynn had been born in Morristown, Ohio, in 1879. The 1900 census listed her as an unemployed teacher, out of work for four months and living with her mother. The odyssey that brought the twenty-plus-year-old to Cleveland remains unknown, but she obviously moved to where the jobs were. Her classroom was in the southwest corner. The fourth occupant of

Pearl P. Lynn's first-grade class in the southwest corner of the first floor. Most of these children would die in the fire. Note how high from the floor the windows are. (Courtesy collinwoodfire.org)

the first floor was Grace Maud Fiske, who taught third grade in the northwest corner. She had come from Penobscot, Maine, where she had been born in 1879 or 1880. In 1900, then nineteen-year-old Grace held a job as a stenographer and lived at home with her parents. The 1907 Cleveland City Directory places her on Orville Avenue.

Laura L. Bodey, the fifth-grade teacher, had been born in England in 1883 and immigrated to the United States with her parents, Walter and Johanna (or simply Anna), in 1888. By the beginning of the 1907–8 academic year, the family resided at 978 Collamer Street, close to the school, and Miss Bodey had been banished to the top floor of the building along with her entire fifth-grade class.

The building's second floor housed an additional third-grade classroom, as well as the second, fourth, and sixth grades. In the southeast corner, Lulu M. Rowley handled the second third-grade class. The twenty-seven-year-old lived on Adams Avenue with her parents. The fourth-grade teacher, Katherine Gollmar, sported perhaps the most interesting background of the nine teachers. Sometimes referred to incorrectly in accounts of the disaster as "Mary Gollmar," Katherine (or Catherine) was born in Germany in 1882 and immigrated to the United States in 1889 at the age of seven. As one of only two foreign-born teachers at the school, chances are she was at minimum bilingual—which would stand her in good stead with at least the German-speaking segment of the immigrant population. Her classroom stood in the building's northwest corner; she lived at 4919 Westropp Avenue. The sixth-grade class, which occupied the room at the northeast corner, remained the purview of Anna R. Moran. Born in Wickliffe, Ohio, in the early 1860s—clearly making her the oldest teacher—Moran, one of the first teachers at the school, doubled as principal. At the time of the fire, she was living on Delaware Avenue with her elderly parents.

We know far more about the background and life of the second-grade teacher, Katherine Weiler, primarily because her father Gustav, a German-born Methodist minister, penned *In Memoriam: Katherine C. Weiler,* dedicated to his daughter after her death in the fire. Born in 1879, the oldest of five children, she was a deeply serious and religious woman. At the ages of four, six, and twelve she apparently experienced some sort of religious ecstasy that led to a childhood of what her father described as "quiet seriousness." She regarded her dolls and other toys not so much as playthings but as treasures that needed her care and attention. As she stood on the brink of her teenage years, she felt, again, according to her father, "full assurance of her acceptance with God." Her devotion to her family was total. When her younger brothers Henry and William left the protective embrace of the Weiler family home and moved to Canton, Ohio, Katherine considered going with them to keep house and protect them from what she saw as the dangerous temptations of the big city.

Devotion to education seemed to run in her blood, even at a young age. When she and her young friends played school, Katherine would invariably take on the role of teacher. In 1895 or 1896, she began postgraduate work in education in Toledo, Ohio, and then at Baldwin Wallace in Berea. Ultimately, she found employment in the small town of North Baltimore, Ohio, about thirty-eight miles from the family home in Toledo. Sometime in 1899 or 1900, she left that position and moved back to her parents' home. (Reverend Weiler maintained that his daughter's days in North Baltimore proved extremely difficult, though he gave no specifics.)

The 1900 census report listed Katherine as an unemployed teacher, out of work for three months; her father does not mention this period of inactivity in his memorial booklet. Her situation would seem to have been identical to that of first-grade teacher Pearl P. Lynn; both were out-of-work teachers in 1900, and both eventually found new jobs near Cleveland in the rapidly growing Collinwood Township. According to the 1907 Cleveland City Directory, Katherine Weiler lived at 297 Clinton in Collinwood; at the time of the disaster she boarded with F. W. Lindow at 2217 East Eighty-First Street.

Her classroom stood in the southwest corner of the school. When the North-Eastern Ohio Teachers' Association held its institute in Cleveland in February 1908, Katherine Weiler was elected "president of the primary department second year." At close to six feet in height, she was a commanding presence in the classroom. Although in her adult years she occasionally showed flashes of humor, which had been almost totally absent during her childhood, she remained rather reserved, only able to express her love for her young pupils in letters home. According to her father, these missives often overflowed with an affection for her pupils that she could not express openly. She often referred to her "Kinder," "Kindets," "bright little Syrians," "smart little Swedes," "mischievous little curly heads," and "sweet little girls." Though she occasionally toyed with the notion of leaving teaching, ultimately she decided education would be her chosen profession. "I believe," she wrote home, "I can do the most good in making teaching my life work."

The 350-plus pupils who gathered in the overcrowded Lakeview School building that fall represented diversity in age, ethnicity, and economic class. Although this was an elementary facility, the oldest pupils in attendance were fifteen, primarily due to difficulties with the English language. In 1907, the school was a mini melting pot whose population mix could rival that of any large American city. Many came from very poor immigrant families that had settled in the area to find work on the railroads or the other industries that had grown up around them. The Bankers' Panic, or Knickerbocker Crisis, of 1907, however, had a devastating economic effect on industrial communities such as Collinwood. Production fell, bankruptcies soared, and what had been a 3 percent unemployment rate nearly tripled. Thus, some pupils who attended Lakeview Elementary School came from households in which the father worked part-time or not at all.

Italian and Slovenian ranked among the neighborhood's dominant native languages, languages that none of the teachers spoke. (Like her colleague Katherine Gollmar, Katherine Weiler spoke German.) "Many of the bereaved families are Greiners," reported the *Plain Dealer* on March 6. "They are poor. They do not know the customs of the land." (*Greiner* refers to Germans and Slovenians of the lower economic classes. Contemporary newspapers often mentioned "Greiner districts" or "Greiner neighborhoods.") In more recent years, some commentators on the Collinwood disaster have tried to make an issue of the gender, age, ethnicity, social position, and probable religious affiliation of the nine teachers—arguing that they were "different" from the majority of their students and that this could have created a gap that negatively affected the teachers' ability to control their students once the fire broke out. Yet the student body also included children from prosperous backgrounds and descendants of the area's original settlers.

Weiler's letters home provide at least a glimpse of the part of that student body with which she dealt daily. She described her students as belonging to the "lowest stratum of social life," and helping some of the more recent immigrants master the complexities of the English language remained one of her top priorities. "During recess my little Hungarian girls gather round me and feel my brooch and comb," she wrote. "Some of them are so untidy, it makes my flesh creep to have them touch me. But they have such a poor home, I have not the heart to deny them the few pleasures they find." When she realized her charges admired her string of pearls, she vowed to wear them more often, because so many of her students rarely saw anything beautiful.

Thanks in part to Marshall Everett's 1908 *Complete Story of the Collinwood School Disaster and How Such Horrors Can Be Prevented*, current notions concerning the actual character and makeup of the student body are, unfortunately, somewhat skewed. He included pictures of approximately fifty pupils who lost their lives in the disaster—less than a third of the 172 killed. In the years since the book's publication, the photos have appeared sporadically in other sources; most recently, they have found a permanent home on several different internet sites. The photographs most likely came from families sufficiently well off to afford formal portraits: girls in lacy white dresses and impossibly large bows atop their heads; boys dressed neatly in little uniforms or children's suits and looking oh so serious while sitting in chairs so large their legs dangled. The students from the "lowest stratum of social life" that Katherine Weiler describes so vividly in her letters are simply not represented, nor are some of the boys in their mid-teens—the poor street kids whom janitor Fritz Hirter occasionally caught hiding in the basement smoking. In the days following the fire, *Press* reporters scoured the neighborhood for photos of the victims to print in the paper. Many of them are of very poor quality and did not make the cut to be included in Everett's book. The overly sentimental wallowing of both his book and the newspaper coverage of the day—as well as some of the cartoons that graced the newspaper stories—create the false impression that every student at the school was a well-behaved cherub somewhere between three and five years old.

. . .

Historical incidents remain a collection of the verifiable facts and recorded utterances that make that event significant, but the mundane details of day-to-day life that run in the background are rarely remembered, precisely because they seem so ordinary. A school invariably becomes a universe unto itself, operating under its own rules and customs. There are so many circumstances about the daily life in Lakeview Elementary School in 1908 that we will probably never know. What was the nature of the relationship between teacher and pupil? What subjects made up the curriculums in the different grades?

How serious were the language barriers between teacher and pupil? What strategies did teachers use to overcome them? How could any young woman deal effectively and maintain discipline with a class of between forty to fifty pupils? How strict were the teachers? Did teachers ever resort to corporal punishment? How did the pupils with poor English skills behave when they had difficulties understanding their teachers? Lulu Rowley maintained that the foreign students were generally more obedient than their native-born counterparts. How much control could a young teacher exercise over her pupils in such large classes during moments of crisis? How well would practice fire drills hold up under extreme duress and panic, especially considering the language barriers? The answers to all these questions form the background against which the disaster in Collinwood unfolded.

. . .

The old adage that March either comes in like a lion and goes out like a lamb or the exact opposite does not always ring true along the shores of Lake Erie. Clevelanders never know what sort of weather to expect in the early days of the month. Daily highs can cover a thirty-degree temperature range, anywhere form the mid-twenties to the low fifties. Snowfalls can be either nonexistent or crippling. In 1908, March entered Cleveland quietly and in a teasing mode, leaving residents wondering about its ultimate metrological intentions. The first few days of the month were cold but not uncomfortably so; temperatures hovered around freezing or slightly above. There had been some sleet on Monday, the second, and Tuesday, the third; but it had been light and didn't stick.

Ash Wednesday, March 4, dawned a tad on the chilly side—around thirty-two degrees, but quiet—no snow on the ground or in the air. On that fateful day, ten-year-old Luella Walden left her home on Elsinore and headed to school still flushed with pride over her new office. A few months before, her third-grade teacher, Miss Grace Fiske, had appointed her "monitor of the fire drill." "I'm to be leader of the pupils in the fire drill, mamma," she had proudly announced when she returned home. "When the gong sounds, I am to jump up and lead the boys and girls out into the schoolyard." There had been at least three fire drills since the beginning of the year, and on these occasions, Luella Walden apparently had performed her assigned duties perfectly—as she no doubt did on the day she died.

NOTES

Mrs. A. P. Burton's reflections on the primitive conditions in Frogsville are preserved in volume 1 of the *Annals of the Early Settlers Association of Cuyahoga County* (1880).

Details of Collinwood's growth have been gleaned from *The Encyclopedia of Cleveland History* and *In Loving Remembrance: The Collinwood School Fire of 1908*, an exhibit prepared by the history and geography department of the Cleveland Public Library. County records contain a number of entries dealing with the evolution of the area ultimately known simply as Collinwood:

1. June 1846: application filed for the formation of East Cleveland Township.
2. Territory taken from Euclid Township added to East Cleveland.
3. August 6, 1866: East Cleveland Village established.
4. November 6, 1872: Glenville Village established.
5. February 3, 1878: part of East Cleveland annexed to Cleveland proper.
6. April 4, 1883: Collinwood Village established out of East Cleveland and Euclid Townships.
7. April 18, 1896: Collinwood Township established out of Collinwood Village.

I am indebted to Elva Brodnick of the Collinwood Nottingham Historical Society for this information.

Passages from Katherine Weiler's letters home are quoted from her father's memorial booklet.

The *Plain Dealer* carried the poignant story of Luella Walden on March 8, 1908.

Chapter Three

MARCH 4, 1908, ASH WEDNESDAY

Fritz Hirter rose before dawn as he did every day of the school year. Most likely Eliza, his wife of sixteen years, stirred when her husband did. (In time, her name would morph into Elizabeth in public documents.) There were eight children in the Hirter household at 447 Collamer Street, and she bore sole responsibility for rousing the brood and readying them all for the day. By 1908, life in the home of the Swiss-German immigrant family had settled into predicable and comfortable routine.

Hirter had come to the United States in 1891, the same year as his future wife, Eliza Wizenreid; they had settled in Cuyahoga County and married the following year. In his native Switzerland, Hirter had tended the boilers at a greenhouse; so once in the United States, it made sense that he would ultimately land a job as janitor at Collinwood's Lakeview Elementary School, where one of his primary responsibilities was tending the building's two large basement furnaces. At forty-three, Fritz Hirter had settled successfully into life along the shores of Lake Erie; he enjoyed both a good job and a large family. By all accounts, he was friendly with the pupils, knowing many of them by their first names. He gave the young male students a penny each for hauling waste paper from the classrooms down to the basement, where they piled it outside the furnaces for future burning. Occasionally, Hirter even allowed some of the boys to help him stoke the fire by throwing in the collected paper and adding coal.

Facing north, the Hirter home stood on the right side of the road; the walk up Collamer to the school was an easy stroll, hardly more than ten minutes. At about 6:30 that morning, Hirter could see the imposing school building looming out of the darkness before him on the left side of the road. As dawn broke and began to spread, he could tell that it would be a clear, sunny day; perhaps, a bit chilly but still. Hirter entered the school through the front doors on the east side of the building and headed to the basement to fire up the two furnaces. The previous day, he had prepared the coal he would need that morning to heat the building. After adding it to the furnaces and stoking the fires, he swept and cleaned the hallways and classrooms—duties he performed every morning before the pupils arrived. It was around 7:30.

Though they may have begun at slightly different times, the morning rituals in the Collinwood households with school-age children, whether rich or poor, American-born or immigrant, unfolded in a remarkably similar fashion: the obligatory washing and dressing, a good breakfast, perhaps some pre-school chores—all followed by gathering up books and supplies, bundling up for the walk to school, and heading out the door armed with motherly kisses and wishes for a good day. Since the Collinwood streets were not paved in 1908, a winter walk to school could be quite an adventure over a bumpy trail of uneven spots, ruts, and mud, as well as the standard seasonal obstacles such as snow, slush, and ice.

Alice Eichelberger ran, worried she might be late. For reasons she could not explain, she was suddenly overcome by a wave of fear, so she turned around and ran home. Fourteen-year-old Angela Skerl should have been at school that day; but because she was the oldest daughter in the household, it was her duty to help her mother with the family baking—even if that meant missing school once in a while. (Her younger sister Pauline would die in the blaze.) Eight-year-old Harry Parr had broken his arm in mid-February, causing him to miss three weeks of school while the break healed. He wanted to stay home on March 4, but his mother—much to her regret—made him go. Four of Fritz Hirter's young children—Helene, Ella, Walter, and Ida—would

Emma Neibert, the fourteen-year-old girl who first noticed the fire during her trip to the restrooms in the basement. (Everett, *Complete Story of the Collinwood School Disaster*)

follow their father's path north on Collamer to the school close to 8:30. At roughly the same time, Emma Neibert and her younger siblings Olga and John left their home on Fifth Street and headed west on Forest Street, toward Collamer and the school. The day's events would permanently change Fritz Hirter's and Emma Neibert's lives—robbing them of children and siblings. Excluding those who were home sick and the few who may have been playing hooky, approximately 350 children headed toward Lakeview Elementary School that morning; 172 would never return.

The day at Lakeview School began officially at either 8:30 or 8:45 (sources differ), so Hirter unlocked the doors to the building sometime between 8:00 and 8:30. Until that moment, Ash Wednesday, March 4, had been a day of utterly normal routine, but all of that would change in slightly more than an hour.

. . .

History is never an exact science; in fact, it is often rather messy—as in the case of Fritz Hirter's encounter with three girls somewhere in the building sometime between 8:00 and 8:30. The official and unofficial statements Hirter made over the next few days differ significantly. In one sense, the discrepancies hardly matter. The incident had no bearing on the horrific events that followed. In addition, considering what Hirter would endure over the next few days—the deaths of three of his own children, burns to his face and hands, and a series of grueling interviews under a variety of circumstances—his subsequent confusion should come as no surprise. The event, however, has always been regarded as an integral part of the Collinwood School Fire story. In one version, Hirter was sweeping the floor when he saw three little girls running through the basement. In a second one, he found the girls hiding in the basement closet where he kept his janitorial supplies sometime between 8:00 and 8:30. In his final and most detailed account, the girls were playing an impromptu game of hide-and-seek and had hidden in a closet, waiting for a fourth girl to find them. When Hirter heard them giggling, he opened the door and shooed them out. Though he did not know their last names, he later identified the trio as Lizzie, Anna, and Mary.

· · ·

The school day began as it always did, with prayer. Sometime between 9:15 and 9:30, Hirter paused in the performance of his daily duties; the building seemed cooler than he had anticipated. The weather over the last few days had been relatively mild for March, so he had kept the boiler fires somewhat lower than the average for that time of year. To correct the situation, he went down to the basement to add more coal to the two furnaces. At roughly the same time, fourteen-year-old Emma Neibert, a fifth grader in Laura Bodey's third-floor classroom, asked permission to go to the restroom. Because the building's only restroom facilities were in the basement, anyone wishing to use them faced a journey down a couple flights of stairs. Emma faced a three-flight descent. She chose the stairs at the front of the building, which faced east, and casually walked down to the lower floors—after all, this was a familiar journey. As she neared the second floor, she could hear the muted sounds of children singing that emanated from Katherine Weiler's second-grade classroom. When she reached the first floor, she froze. Something was wrong! Smoke was curling up through the cracks in the wooden stairs.

. . .

The alarm sounded at 9:30. In all nine classrooms, the students automatically and calmly rose from their desks, lined up at the classroom doors, and prepared to march down the stairs in orderly fashion to exit the building. This was old stuff for most of them—a simple fire drill. Sixth-grade teacher and school principal Anna Moran, however, knew something had gone awry the moment she heard the alarm. "I realized at once that something had gone wrong because I always gave the signal for fire drills myself," she told the *Press* on March 6. First-grade teacher Ruby Irwin also sensed immediately that this was not a normal fire drill. The rope that activated the alarm was in her classroom in the northeast corner of the building, and official procedure dictated that either Superintendent Frank P. Whitney or Principal Moran would enter the room and pull it. But she hadn't seen either do so; the man who rushed into her classroom to sound the alarm was janitor Fritz Hirter.

. . .

The moment Emma Neibert noticed the smoke rising from the stairs, she called to Hirter, whom she saw sweeping around the furnaces, that something was on fire. Due either to the distance between the two or to the volume level of Emma's voice, Hirter apparently didn't hear her initial warning. When she called to him a second time, he looked up and saw the wisp of smoke—what he would later describe as nothing more than what one would see coming from a lit cigar, while Neibert insisted she saw a lot of smoke.

Initially, Hirter wasn't sure what he should do. He had never sounded the fire alarm before; it was not part of his job. During fire drills, Hirter had been instructed to open the doors to the building at both the east

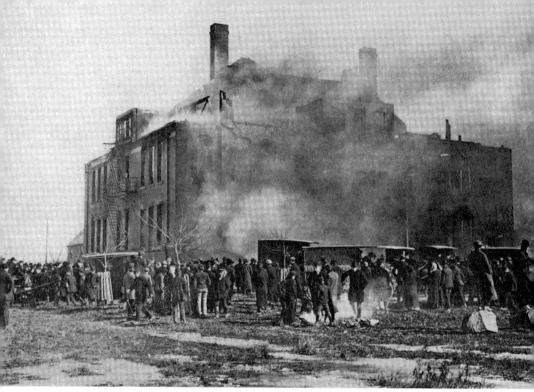

The rapidly growing fire quickly consumed the school's wooden interior. (Everett, *Complete Story of the Collinwood School Disaster*)

and west ends after Anna Moran or Frank Whitney sounded the alarm. Clearly, though, this was not a drill! Hirter dashed past the girl, telling her to get out of the building, and then ran into Ruby Irwin's first-grade classroom, where he rang the fire alarm three times. When he saw his five-year-old daughter sitting in a corner of the room, he shouted to her, "Hurry Ella! Go home!" She thus became the only Hirter child out of the four at the school to survive the fire. Emma Neibert testified later that night at the investigation called by the school board. "Mr. Hirter ran and sounded the bell," she explained. "I ran out the front of the building and didn't see him again. I opened one side of the door and hooked it back. Just one side of the door was open. The inside doors were open. . . . I put the hook on the string on the handle of the door." Hirter later contradicted Emma Neibert's testimony, insisting that he had opened all the doors. Though opening the front and rear doors to facilitate escape would seem the proper thing to do, in retrospect, the action proved a disastrous mistake. The northeast winds blew through the opened front doors, creating a chimney effect that would radically hasten the development of the rapidly growing fire.

. . .

Virtually everything known about the horrendous conditions inside the burning building comes from testimony provided by the surviving teachers and janitor Fritz Hirter, given at either the subsequent coroner's inquest or school board inquiry. The evacuation procedure during fire drills was based on logic and relied on efficiency, discipline, and timing. Theoretically, when the alarm sounded, the pupils on all three floors would line up in their respective classrooms at the same time, leave their rooms with their teachers as guides, head for their designated stairway to exit the building, and, depending on the position of their classrooms in relation to the stairs, march down either the right or left side of the staircase. They were to head directly out of the building without stopping in the cloakroom. The younger children, on the bottom floor, would leave the building first, through either the east or west exit. Just as they were filing through the doors, the lines of older students from the second and third floors would be descending the stairs, the front of their lines falling directly behind those of the younger children. In a moment of crisis, so much depended on the amount of control the teachers could exercise and their pupils' willingness to obey.

Once it started, the blaze grew and spread at an almost unbelievably ferocious rate. Emma Neibert had spotted the initial evidence of the fire, perhaps literally within moments of it having started, and Hirter had sounded the alarm immediately. Yet within minutes, the flames had grown to such an extent that they had begun to consume at least a part of the stairs under which they had started. Though her class was a new one and had reportedly never been through a fire drill, kindergarten teacher Ethel Rose was the first to get her pupils safely out of the building. (If there had been a fire drill as late as January or early February, how could Ethel Rose's class have possibly missed it? It was, however, a kindergarten class, and designated as "new."

Apparently, kindergarten classes operated on a different schedule from the rest of the building, possibly having something to do with the children's ages and their perceived inability to concentrate for as long as their elder schoolmates.)

"I was standing at the blackboard," Ethel Rose later recalled, according to the March 6 *News*, "with one section of my pupils who were all of the lower first grade, when the gong rang very rapidly." As she led her class from her southeast corner room into the central hall, she saw thick smoke rolling out of the basement. Although she did not notice flames, she ordered her children to run as quickly as possible to the east exit. About half of her thirty-one pupils had gotten safely out of the building before the flames began to roar up between the banister and the hall stairs. Fearing some of her remaining young charges might panic and, in their confusion, run to the basement steps, she effectively blocked them by positioning herself at the head of the stairway. When a couple fell on their way down the stairs to the exit, she scooped them up and made sure they escaped. Ethel Rose and most of her kindergartners were lucky; they managed to get out of the building before the rapidly expanding blaze completely blocked the front doors.

At approximately the same moment as Rose was hustling her pupils toward the east exit and safety, Ruby Irwin and Pearl Lynn were leading their first graders out of their respective first-floor rooms. The moment Lynn opened the door of her classroom in the southwest corner, the smoke poured in. When they saw the smoke, Irwin's pupils broke ranks almost immediately; they rushed desperately to the eastern exit, where approximately half managed to escape before the flames and heat completely blocked the doors and drove those remaining back toward the center of the building, where they ultimately joined the now panicking mob of Lynn's pupils rushing to the western exit. According to Edward Kern, she later testified that her students, "were in good order until they smelled smoke." The surge of panicked children behind her pushed her violently forward, down to the foot of the stairs, where she sprawled on top of students who had already stumbled, only to be crushed by the hysterical children behind her rushing to the western exit.

Irwin struggled mightily to restore a sense of order by redirecting the remaining students back to their respective classrooms, where they could be lowered out of the windows to rescuers who had already arrived at the burning building. As with many older schools, the windows on the first story were high off the floor and even higher from the ground outside. In their fear and confusion, a number of children hesitated to make the seven-to-eight-foot leap and had to be coaxed into the arms of waiting rescuers.

Third-grade teacher Grace M. Fiske occupied the fourth classroom on the first floor, in the building's northwest corner. None of the existing accounts specifies the point at which she and her class joined the worsening situation in the school's central open mall area, but the fact that order and discipline were already collapsing would suggest she may have been the last of the four teachers on the first floor to leave her classroom. She seems to have immediately joined her three colleagues in the struggle to keep some sense of calm and order among their young pupils. The oft-practiced orderly evacuation procedure, however, was crumbling, though it had not yet disintegrated into the chaos of blind panic. But the students from the top two floors, numbering more than two hundred, were hurrying down the staircases to the first floor: to the smoke, the flames, and a blocked exit.

. . .

Within ten minutes of the alarm, fourteen-year-old Clarence Scholl had the presence of mind to get out of the building through a first-floor classroom window and run across the street to a school supply store, where he phoned Collinwood's Chief of Police Charles G. McIlrath at the town hall. The chief immediately sounded the general alarm, ran outside, stopped a passing wagon, and ordered the driver to the take him to the school. Three of his children were in the burning building! Since the fire alarm only sounded in the school itself, it isn't entirely clear how Collinwood's meager fire department of twenty men got the summons. Once alerted, however, the strictly volunteer department coped with what seemed an unending chain of obstructions. The horses that pulled the antiquated equipment were not in their barn; they had been loaned to village workers to pull a road scraper somewhere at the south end of Collinwood, far from the burning school. There was simply no way of retrieving them. Precious minutes also passed while the men hitched a team borrowed from the livery stable next door to the equipment wagon. Not used to hauling heavy firefighting gear, the commandeered team consistently resisted the driver's efforts to make them move more quickly and slowed down considerably while crossing the huge arc of the bridge that spanned the sprawling railroad yards; once on the other side, the wheels of the wagon sank into ankle-deep mud. The growing fire had consumed a major portion of the building by the time the volunteer team finally arrived at the school, only to be hampered further by abnormally low water pressure producing weak and largely ineffective streams of water, leaky old hoses, and twenty-foot ladders that could reach no higher than the windows of the first floor. Forty men from the private Lake Shore fire department reached the site six minutes after the Collinwood volunteers; but, according to Chief Joseph Jones, the

The hook and ladder of Collinwood's volunteer fire department. The ladders were not long enough to reach the building's upper floors. (Everett, *Complete Story of the Collinwood School Disaster*)

Fighting the fire at its height. Note that the fire hoses cannot reach beyond the school's first floor. The photograph shows the west exit of the building, where most of the children died. (Courtesy The Cleveland *Press* Collection, Michael Schwartz Library, Cleveland State University)

constant press around his men by the growing mob of spectators made it extremely difficult for them to work.

. . .

The ringing alarm bell caught fifth-grade teacher Laura Bodey off guard. She had only been at the school for a few weeks; though her students were familiar with the evacuation routine, she had never been through a fire drill. Her more than forty pupils, however, lined up as they had always practiced, filed out of their third-floor classroom, and marched toward the stairs, only to be assailed by the smoke and heat before they reached the second floor. Realizing that escape via the practiced route had become impossible, her pupils began to panic and break ranks. Somehow, Bodey kept a semblance of order and steered most of her class to a small second-floor window that opened on to the school's sole fire escape. While the fire escape had never figured before in evacuation practice, Bodey saved most of her class. Like most external fire escapes, its iron steps did not reach to the ground. The structure had never been supplied with a downfall—a piece that swings to the ground from the last step when the escape is being used. Facing a drop of over eight feet, many of her pupils were at first reluctant to leap into the arms of waiting rescuers below. (Some children actually leapt from the second-story and third-story windows only to be killed by the fall.) Sixty years later, a former student identified only as Mrs. E. W. of Euclid told the *Plain Dealer,* "My teacher Miss Laura Bodey, now deceased, deserved a gold medal. There were about 50 children in my 5A class, and 14 broke line and ran down the stairway never to be seen again. I owe my life to Miss Bodey."

Katherine Gollmar's fourth-grade students rose from their desks at the sound of the alarm, lined up, and filed out of their northwest classroom. When Lulu Rowley heard the alarm, she was in the middle of a geography lesson. She promptly ordered one of her pupils at the back of the room to open the classroom door as her third graders lined up and prepared to leave. The moment the unnamed student carried out her command, black smoke rolled into the room. Someone yelled, "Fire!" On March 6, the *Press* ran a brief article supposedly written by Lulu Rowley: "It was when smoke poured into the room that I realized that this was more serious than our ordinary fire drill." When Anna Moran heard the bell, she at first sensed no danger—even though she knew something had gone wrong, since neither she nor the school superintendent had sounded the alarm. "I thought that everyone would have ample time to reach a place of safety," she told the *Press* on March 6. "Children from the floors above began marching by the door [to her classroom]. They did not seem excited. I accompanied the children in my room down the hall." But the situation deteriorated immediately. On March 5, the *News* recounted Anna Moran's vivid testimony before the school board. "I told the children to form in line, but they were so frightened they would not. The children in the other rooms were screaming. There came a frightened roar from the children in my room and they rushed past me. I could not control them. They knocked me from my feet. I screamed at them to come back, but it was useless. They could not hear me and would not have minded if they could have heard."

What started as an orderly exit from the burning school collapsed within minutes into a chaotic nightmare: the shrieking and screaming mobs of panicked children surging to the exits, the pleading and shouting teachers desperate to steer their charges to safety, the smoke-filled hallways, the incredible heat of the rapidly spreading fire, the frantic efforts of parents, neighbors, and other rescuers outside the building. By all accounts, the breakdown began on the first floor, among the younger students. Perhaps they thought the evacuation routine had simply become an exercise to be repeated at regular intervals, a mandatory procedure that bore no relationship to anything real. The moment the children realized that the school was actually on fire, any memory of an orderly evacuation immediately dissolved into panic; and despite their best efforts, the four teachers—Ethel Rose, Pearl Lynn, Ruby Irwin, and Grace Fiske—were unable to reassert much control.

Roughly a quarter to a third of the children on the first floor got out of the building before the growing fire blocked the east exit completely. Some ran home, while others stayed to watch. (Emma Neibert went home but returned to the scene with her mother.) Through sheer force of will, Ruby Irwin redirected some of the pupils back into their classrooms and ultimately to safety out of the first-floor windows; but most of the frightened children broke ranks and disintegrated into a desperate, disorganized mob running frantically toward the west exit. Inevitably, some of them stumbled and fell, only to be trampled by the human wave behind them; many of the students died of suffocation or were simply crushed to death. When some children tripped over those who had already fallen, they became a writhing mass struggling toward what they perceived as the only remaining means of escape.

The rapidly deteriorating situation plunged into total chaos when the older students from the second floor reached the stairs leading to the ground floor. "I realized that escape was impossible in that direction [the east exit] and I called to the children to follow me upstairs to the fire escape," Anna Moran testified at the coroner's inquest on March 6. "Few of them heeded me. They seemed to think they were nearer to safety on the first floor and rushed wildly forward." Similarly, Lulu Rowley recalled, "At the foot of the stairs the passage through the front door was cut off by the flames. I called to my class to file into one of the rooms on the first floor. Only a few obeyed." Anna Moran and Katherine Gollmar tried to stop the wave struggling toward the rear door and redirect the children to the library on the second floor and ultimately to the fire escape. "We took back a number, how many I don't know," Moran testified according to the *Press* on March 7. "We took them into the room and Miss Gollmar pulled a table away from the window leading to the fire escape." After Anna Moran smashed the window with a chair, "the children and Miss Gollmar went down that." After checking to see if there were any students left on the second floor, Moran struggled through the blinding smoke back to the fire escape and to safety. Out of her thirty-one students, only six survived.

Ruby Irwin joined Lulu Rowley in her attempt to drive the panicked children into one of the first-floor classrooms. "To the windows, children," she shouted; but none would obey her. "I grabbed some, lifted some, drove some into a room"—the same room into which Lulu Rowley had led a portion of her class. "Miss Rowley had taken some into the room," she recalled according to the *Press*. "All who were in the room were saved. Miss Rowley stood in a window and I lifted them up to her and she dropped them to the ground." If any of the children hesitated to leap to safety, Lulu Rowley pushed them. "We were unable to leave the room except by jumping from a window," Ruby Irwin insisted.

The stark realization that the school was actually on fire completely shattered any sense of order among the students. The neat lines of pupils descending the stairs collapsed immediately into a human wave pushing violently forward, crushing and trampling everything in its path. Since Katherine Weiler died in the fire and Grace Fiske succumbed to her burns in Glenville Hospital shortly after her rescue, the very little that is known about their actions during the chaos of the evacuation comes from secondhand sources. Weiler was leading her second-grade pupils from her second-floor classroom to the top of the back stairs when she saw the flames blocking the east exit, the swirling smoke, and the breakdown in order on the first floor. She tried vainly to stop her charges and force them back to the second floor and the fire escape, but the wildly spreading panic proved too great. She waded through the mass of screaming children and succeeded in getting a few to the safety of the fire escape. Reportedly, her powerful voice desperately urging calm literally soared over the welter of confusion. She reached the fire escape, but rather than saving herself, she struggled back into the maelstrom only to be trampled by the frantic crush pushing down the staircase. When the plunging mob completely clogged the bottom of the stairs, some students leapt over the bannister, only to fall on top of the prostrate mass of younger children struggling toward the rear exit. Some tried to walk or run over the writhing, hysterically screaming pile of younger schoolmates; others crawled or actually tried to "swim" over a living tangle of children. One survivor reported witnessing young children screaming in pain and trying to smother the fires in their hair with their hands as he clawed his way over them.

The building's design became one of the major impediments. At the east and west ends of the building, there were two sets of doors—an inner set, attached to partitions, leading into a small foyer or vestibule, and the outer set. At the foot of the rear stairs leading to the west exit, the left inner door was bolted to the top of the frame by a spring lock, leaving only the right door, less than three feet wide open, leading into the small hallway. When a few of the younger children stumbled, those behind them continued to push forward, trying to crawl to safety over fellow schoolmates now jamming the doorway. But utter panic reigned. The older students stumbled over the struggling younger ones, ultimately forming a frantic wedge that completely blocked the doorway. When members of the growing crowd of neighborhood rescuers reached the inner set of doors at the west exit, they literally confronted a stack of tightly packed screaming children completely plugging the doorway from top to bottom, their arms reaching out, begging for rescue.

· · ·

When the alarm bell sounded in the school at 9:30, those residents closest to the school building heard it, and they immediately left home and began rushing to the burning building. At least some of the newspaper accounts of neighbors rushing to the school the moment the alarm sounded probably are overdramatized. Since school authorities regularly held fire drills, why would anyone respond merely to the sound of the alarm—unless signs of the blaze, such as smoke, were evident almost immediately?

Florence Sprung lived at 382 Collamer Street, only two doors north of the school. Whether she reacted only to the alarm or saw the early signs of the fire remains unknown, but she was apparently one of the first on the scene. She ran to the school with a short ladder and threw it up against the outer wall, but it only reached as high as the windows of the first floor. A teacher—most likely Ruby Irwin—was trying vainly to restore some vestige of calm amid a hysterical crowd of panicked children, among whom the distraught woman saw her seven-year-old son, Alvin. She called to him and then watched helplessly as the struggling mass of children forced him out of the classroom into the smoke-filled hallway. She never saw him again.

A woman identified only as Mrs. Rostock of 5315 Lake Avenue was ironing when she heard the alarm. Deeply concerned for two of her five children—fourteen-year-old Emil and six-year-old Lillian, she dropped her iron and ran to the school in her bare feet over the rough, partly frozen ground. Neither child survived. Desperately worried about the safety of her three children, Mrs. Paul Gordon also ran frantically toward the school. (Only her daughter Ruth died in the flames.) When Joseph Neil's wife saw the smoke and screamed that the schoolhouse was on fire, he rushed from their Ridpath Avenue home to the north side of building and stationed himself beneath the fire escape. He saved more than twenty children, who leaped into his arms from either the fire escape or the first-floor windows.

Word of the developing catastrophe at Lakeview Elementary School spread rapidly through the tightly packed Collinwood community. Those few residents who lived close to the school and had responded to the alarm almost immediately were joined by parents, neighbors, police, members of the volunteer fire department, shopkeepers, factory workers, and railroad men—even a small group of linemen from the Cuyahoga Telephone Company, installing lines about block from the school—all of whom rushed to the burning building. On March 5, the *Plain Dealer* carried the poignant story of a gray-haired man who fell to his knees in the mud and moaned, "Oh, God, what have we done to deserve this?" Some women rushing to the scene dropped to their knees beside him and bent their heads in prayer. Public and official response to the alarm had been nearly instantaneous; rescue still seemed possible.

An event of overwhelming chaotic horror involving several hundred people can never be reduced to a single story with beginning, middle, and end. The historical record recounting the few hours the Collinwood School Fire raged remains a jumble of separate accounts that defy strict chronological order, describing the actions and ultimate fates of children, teachers, parents, police, firefighters, and rescuers. Together, the accounts weave a complex tapestry of stories and fragments of stories—individual snapshots of heroism and heartbreak caught during a massive storm of unimaginable horror and violence: Mildred Schmidt, running from the building screaming, her clothes afire (she would later die at the hospital); Glen Sanderson, trapped on the third floor trying to make his way to the fire escape by swinging from pieces of scenery—stored in the attic-cum-fifth-grade classroom—that were hanging from the ceiling, only to lose his grip and fall into the inferno below; John Pazicky, killed when he ran back into the doomed building to retrieve his red cap.

The moment news of the fire reached city newspaper offices, reporters for all of Cleveland's newspapers immediately rushed to the scene. The *Plain Dealer* scored a major victory over its competition when Robert Scholl, manager of the Lake Shore Land Company, offered his office as a base of operations; thus, newspaper staff transported typewriters and other publishing paraphernalia to the neighborhood satellite office. For the rest of that terrible day, reporters moved through the swelling crowd, miners panning for journalistic gold.

Frank J. Dorn, a member of the school board and chairman of its building committee, was in the kitchen when the alarm sounded.

One of the first to arrive at the school, he and Collinwood patrolman Charles L. Wahl reached the rear door before it became clogged with frantic children. "The fire had not got much headway when we reached the school," he reported. "The flames were burning in the front part of the hall and had shut off escape from that way, but the rear entrance was still free and children were pouring out. I went to the west door. I first found a little girl lying 10 or 12 feet from the building, with her head battered, her clothes burning. I carried her a little way and gave her to some women." Dorn saw the first child trip and fall in the doorway and watched in horror as the sheer force of humanity pushed forward, children trampling and stumbling over their prostrate schoolmate. He and Wahl dragged a number of children to safety before the doorway became impassable. "I could see my little girl [Gretchen] in the rear of the crowd," he recalled. "She was with Blanch McIlrath [her name was actually Viola May], chief McIlrath's daughter [Charles McIlrath of the Collinwood Police]. I called to them to come on and I would pull them over the heap of children. I saw them turn and go up the stairway. That was the last I saw of my girl." Viola May McIlrath survived the fire; Gretchen Dorn did not.

Twenty-four-year-old John Leffel lived near the school and was thus one of the first on the scene. "I ran to the school when I saw the smoke. The rear entrance, where the storm doors blocked up the arch, was heaped up with little bodies. Some of the children seemed half suffocated. Some were unconscious." When Harry Sigler got to the building, he saw, "a little girl lying under one of the windows. I turned her over and saw that her face was all crushed in." Real estate agent Henry Ellis left his home on Westropp Avenue and headed to the burning school when he heard a boy running down the street shouting, "Fire!" He and Lake Shore roundhouse superintendent L. E. Cross arrived at the rear door, where they joined Dorn and Wahl in pulling as many children as they could from the doomed building, mostly from the top of the struggling heap forming in the doorway. "It was the most heartrending sight I ever saw," Ellis told the *Plain Dealer*. "They were crowded in, one on top of the other, as a cord of wood is piled up. The fire swept on through the hall. It sprang from one child to another, catching in their hair and the girls' dresses. The cries of those in the rear were heart rending." Ellis remained at the doorway, frantically trying to save as many children as he could, until the ravaging heat blistered his face and hands.

Collinwood resident Mathew O'Hearn worked diligently alongside Ellis until the scorching heat drove him back from the doorway. "The children were piled up just like cordwood to a height of more than six feet," he told the *Press*. "It doesn't seem possible that they could have become wedged in as they were, and I could hardly have believed it if I had not seen them." Collinwood patrolman Charles L. Wahl also testified that he tried unsuccessfully to pull children out of the human wedge jamming the door, "but it was of no use. I couldn't move one of them. Three times I tried to get them, but the heat was too great. It was terrible. The fire was coming out over the children in a solid wall. As I think of it now, I can't remember hearing them scream, although I remember the awful pain reflected in their faces."

Mrs. Walter C. Kelly also recalled an eerie silence. "They were silent, most of them. The heat had become so intense when I arrived that they were stifling and their agonized screams were stilled. The hair of most of the children was burned off, their clothes were afire; their faces, upturned, were glazed over by the furious blast of flame which poured over their heads." "Their eyes—that's what I see all the time; that's what I never can forget," moaned Wallace Upton." Joe Curran saw the rising smoke from the backyard of his Collamer Street home. When he reached the rear exit of the school, he saw his young son Paul struggling among the mass of children wedged in the doorway. "He knew me," Curran lamented. "He called to me 'Papa, help me.' I had hold of him. I put out the fire in his hair. I pulled his arms out of their sockets. And I could not save him."

William Davis of Westropp Avenue repeatedly threw himself against the closed door, trying to dislodge it, until something falling from above stunned him. Somehow Lake Shore shopman Frank Durham managed to grab teacher Pearl Lynn by the arm and pull her free from the human tangle—her clothes torn to pieces, her body badly burned, but alive. Railroad worker John Warren shimmied up a drainpipe into one of the first-floor classrooms and managed to save three children, presumably by taking them to the windows.

Before the intense heat drove them back, Robert Golloway, Wallace Upton, August Hausrath, and John Leffel pulled children from the top of the pile forming in the rear doorway and literally tossed them to safety. Hausrath then ran around to the side of the building just as fourteen-year-old Cora Zimmerman jumped from a first-floor window, hitting him on the shoulder. Neither sustained serious injury. Hausrath stood under the first-floor windows and caught six children brave enough to make the leap. Upton somehow got inside the building and into one of the first-floor classrooms, where he dropped children from the windows to the arms of rescuers. After saving eighteen, he collapsed and had to be carried from the building, suffering severe burns. Physicians were forced to dress his wounds on the scene because he refused to go to the hospital. His injuries, however, were so severe newspapers predicted his death was most likely imminent. (Upton, however, died in 1932 at the age of sixty-four.)

Ten-year-old Glen Barber saved himself by kicking out a window and crying to the men standing below: "Catch me! Catch me!" Mrs. John Phillis of Poplar Street learned of the fire when her four-year-old son innocently called out, "Oh, mamma, look at the children playing on the fire escape." She ran to the building, only to be pushed back by other frantic mothers struggling to reach the west exit doors. Miraculously, the desperate mother got close enough to grab her fourteen-year-old daughter Emma Jane "Jennie" by the arms but was unable to extricate her from the struggling mass of children plugging the doorway. Before the heat drove her back, she held Jennie's hand while trying to brush the flames away from her head. A heavy piece of falling glass, however, drove her back, her hand burned to the bone and now cut and bleeding.

For a few precious minutes, parents and rescuers struggled successfully to pull children from the top of the growing pile threatening to completely block the doorway; but the working space was too narrow and the human crush from inside was simply too great. After successfully leading her kindergarten class from the growing inferno, Ethel Rose raced around the building to the west end where she joined the frenzied crowd trying to force open the latched door. "I pulled at it, but I couldn't open it," she reported, according to the *News* on March 6. "I saw that the flames had reached the heads of the children. The children were piled up 10 deep when I got there, several feet from the door. . . . Miss Lynn was underneath the pile, and I pulled at her but could not move her." When Rose's hair caught fire, she retreated to beat it out, only to be grabbed around the waist and swung aside when she tried to return. Men beat on the closed door with their fists until their hands bled. Incredibly, the volunteer fire department had arrived without any axes, and a frantic search through the neighborhood for one came up empty.

After Fritz Hirter turned on the alarm, he ran back into the open mall area where he "saw the flames shooting all about and the little children running down through them screaming." He dashed into one of the first-floor rooms and began lifting children to the windows. When he saw the frantic crush of students blocking the rear door, he ran outside to the west exit and joined the desperate parents struggling in vain to extricate their children from the rapidly growing inferno by pulling on their outstretched arms—working until the flames had burned his face and arms. "I saw my own little Helena among them. I tried to pull her out, but the flames drove me back. I had to leave my little child to die."

After failing to extricate his eight-year-old son, George, from the writhing tangle, W. C. Schaeffer stood protectively by the small boy, holding his hand and comforting him as the flames approached. Men from the neighborhood stood outside the building holding out their arms, shouting for children to jump from the windows. Few were willing to take the risk. As the fire grew and the precious minutes wore on, it became painfully obvious that not all those who joined the swelling crowds around the burning building were frantic parents or determined rescuers.

· · ·

The fire spread through the entire first floor with ferocious and terrible rapidity. Katherine Gollmar and Ethel Rose would later testify that any escape from the bottom floor became virtually impossible within two and a half to three minutes. When school superintendent Frank P. Whitney reached the building around 10:10, only forty minutes after the fire began, the blaze was already far advanced. "The building was then a mass of flames," he recounted at the coroner's inquest on March 6. "I could not see any children in the rear doorway, it being hidden by smoke and fire."

At 10:16, Chief George A. Wallace of the Cleveland fire department responded to a "still alarm" and dispatched Engine Company 30 (from

The final stages of the fire. Ambulances were at the scene of the disaster. This photograph shows the school's sole fire escape on the north side of the building. (Courtesy of the Cleveland Public Library Photograph Collection)

East 105th Street and St. Clair Avenue), a 1904 American Steamer fire engine, an 1895 ladder truck, and a hose truck—all under the command of Battalion Chief Michael F. Fallon. Firefighter John O'Brien left the West 4th Street and St. Clair Station in a borrowed car, steadying the department's giant safety net on the roof of the car with one hand as he drove. When the horse pulling the conveyance in which Fallon rode threw a shoe close to East 105th, he immediately commandeered a passing automobile to complete the journey east, arriving at the school about 10:50—an hour and twenty minutes after the alarm had been sounded.

Shortly before the Cleveland reinforcements got to the scene, a gust of wind from the open eastern doors sent a wall of flame toward the west exit, where so many of the students were piled up; the contingent of rescuers and the massive crowd of onlookers watched in disbelief and utter horror as the first floor—to be quickly followed by the entire interior of the burning building—collapsed into the basement with a huge roar accompanied by a giant plume of smoke and flame billowing above the ruins. The burning debris plunged into the basement, taking with it all the students who still crowded the stairs and packed the rear doorway. Echoing Superintendent Whitney's observations, Fallon later wrote in his report, "The building was doomed, nothing remained but the four walls." The assembled firefighters still aimed five weak streams of water from their leaky hoses at the smoldering ruins, principally the wooden partitions in the basement that continued to burn. Fallon ordered three of the teams to abandon their futile efforts, leaving only two groups of men working at the rear of the ruins to wash away the debris from the burned bodies still piled at what had been the rear interior doors.

. . .

News of the terrible disaster in Collinwood spread rapidly throughout the entire Cleveland area, attracting an estimated crowd of twenty-five thousand onlookers, whom the *Plain Dealer* branded as "morbid curiosity seekers" on March 5. The *News* concurred the next day with an article by Edna K. Wooley titled "Morbid Vultures Prey Upon Grief."

An unnamed *Plain Dealer* writer indignantly described long lines of cars and carriages streaming slowly down Collamer in both directions, their drivers and passengers hoping to get a good look at the unfolding tragedy. "The mud around the building was a foot deep," the author declared, "but it did not deter the thousands of morbid men and women from walking and standing around in it for hours." "There is untold grief in Collinwood today," raged Wooley in the *News*. "There is also sincere sympathy among Collinwood's neighbors for the stricken village. But there are those who are proving themselves thoroughly inhuman by failing to respect the sorrow and by intruding upon the

Part of the crowd that gathered at the west end of the building once the fire was almost out. (Courtesy findagrave.com)

privacy of the bereaved." She noted with disgust that most of those who were there "simply out of morbid curiosity" were women. Dubbing them "vultures of grief," Wooley angrily told her readers how some women tramped through the houses of the bereaved, their shoes caked with mud from standing around the doomed building. When asked if she were a relative, one startled intruder replied, "Oh, my no. I come from the other end of the city. I don't live in Collinwood." Reporters watched incredulously as the curious onlookers invaded the porches of nearby houses and even climbed to the roofs to get a better look at the unfolding disaster.

The *Plain Dealer* noted derisively that the developing catastrophe had attracted both professional and amateur photographers—even someone with a motion picture camera—who kept working as long as there was enough light. In a desperate and largely unsuccessful attempt to keep the huge crowds from hampering the rescue and recovery efforts, a contingent of twelve Collinwood policemen tried to rope off the area around the burning school by establishing a fire line. Unfortunately, there was almost no way for the small force of lawmen to distinguish between agonized parents and the morbidly curious. The massive intrusion of insensitive onlookers remains perhaps the most underreported aspect of the Collinwood tragedy.

But some of the onlookers were clearly there to offer assistance and whatever shreds of comfort they could. A reporter from the *Plain Dealer* noticed a well-dressed woman in the crowd obviously trying, rather unsuccessfully, to comfort some of the grieving mothers. "My son Walter and myself were coming from Conneaut on the train this morning and saw the fire from the window," reported Jeannette Appleby. They had arrived on the scene just as the first ambulances were pulling up. "I shall never forget those agonized mothers," she lamented, "and there were so few that could understand us when we tried to give them a word of comfort."

One onlooker especially attracted the *Press*'s attention—a stately, exceedingly elegant woman who clearly stood out among the gawkers jockeying for position. The former Clevelander, born Belle Platt, now bore the title Countess Gian Francesco Di Castelvetro. "Yes, I'm a countess," she explained to reporters. "But what does that matter? I know what sorrow is. I've had it and I want to help." Belle Platt's personal odyssey from average Clevelander to Italian countess is worthy of a romance novel. After a happy childhood in Cleveland, she joined an opera company in New York, where she met and married the count whose name she bore, only to have him desert her after a few months. Her subsequent mental breakdown earned her a brief stay in Bellevue Hospital.

Upon recovery, the countess returned to Cleveland, armed with a profound sense of civic duty. Ignoring the mud and grime that passing vehicles splattered on her clothes, she now stood at the scene of the disaster performing what acts of charity she could for the bereaved, such as providing black velvet attire for a poor woman who had nothing to wear to her children's funeral and promising a grieving mother that she would babysit her surviving children so she could attend the funeral of the two who had died. "Sorrow Makes Countess Kin of Poor and Humble; Tries to Cheer Stricken," proclaimed the headline of a laudatory article—complete with picture of the imposing woman—in the *Press* on March 7.

. . .

Virtually all the existing accounts of the catastrophe focus on the total breakdown of order among the students during the evacuation procedure—the blind, all-consuming panic that led to children being trampled by their schoolmates, desperate to escape the growing fire. There were, however, tales of genuine heroism among these accounts of selfish—though eminently understandable—desperation. "I saw the big boys trying to help the little girls," ran the report in the *Plain Dealer* on March 6. "They could have got out if they had jumped out of the windows, but they tried to help until it was too late." On March 6, the *Plain Dealer* told the poignant story of fourteen-year-old James Turner who, having saved himself, ran back into the inferno to rescue his two younger brothers Norman (age nine) and Maxwell (age six). All three were killed.

. . .

J. J. Bennet, general superintendent of the Lake Shore Railroad, and M. D. Franey, superintendent of the Lake Shore shops, immediately emerged as true heroes of the Collinwood disaster. As Collinwood's major employer, the railroad industry had to be constantly on guard and prepared to deal with any catastrophe that might occur, such as an exploding engine or a fire; therefore, both men knew exactly what to do and responded to the alarm immediately, truly becoming men of the hour. Within fifteen minutes of the alarm, Bennet wired village clerk John F. Murray: "Call me for money or other aid that may be needed." He then ordered Franey to dispatch Lake Shore's private fire department, along with the full workforce of the railroad shops armed with picks, shovels, and such vitally necessary supplies as stretchers and blankets. When the recovery effort began, there was no place to take the bodies, so Lake Shore provided a company storehouse to be turned into a temporary morgue under the watchful eyes of Cuyahoga County's Coroner Thomas A. Burke and Deputy Coroner O'Neil. None of the city newspapers ever pinpointed the exact location of the storehouse. No address was given; no street name was even specified. A 1912 plat map of the area shows the entire massive, sprawling Lake Shore complex just north of the railroad lines and east of Collamer/East 152nd. The most likely structure is a rather small storehouse that lies slightly southwest of the huge locomotive machine shop.

Calls also went out for ambulances to take the seriously injured to the hospital and undertakers' wagons to transport the dead to the Lake Shore storehouse. Police Chief McIlrath had arrived on the scene almost immediately after the alarm had sounded. Three of his own children—Hugh, fourteen; Viola May, nine; and Benson, seven—attended the school. For the next six hours, without knowing whether his children were alive or dead, McIlrath struggled with the men of his department to keep the rapidly growing crowd of frantic parents and insensitive spectators back so the firemen and rescuers could work unhampered. At one point, he glanced up to the top of the fire escape and caught a glimpse of Hugh apparently helping younger children negotiate the dangers of the iron stairway. Suddenly, however, he was gone. It wasn't until late in the day that the worried father learned that while Benson

The school building's devastated interior. The photograph shows the two furnaces in the basement. The eastern exit of the building can be seen at the upper left. Since the fire began almost directly beneath the eastern exit, it became impassible almost immediately. (Everett, *Complete Story of the Collinwood School Disaster*)

and Viola May had survived the ordeal, Hugh had not. "It's Hughie," he muttered sadly upon recognizing his son's body at the Lake Shore shop. After wiping away a tear, he returned to the smoldering ruin and stood on guard well into the night.

. . .

By 1:30 P.M., the massive blaze had largely burned itself out, save for a few hot spots. The appalling task of recovering the victims began around 3:30, and the official tone of Cleveland fire department battalion chief Michael F. Fallon's official report—issued at day's end—reveals the sheer horror of such grueling and sickening work. "Under my supervision the men worked with shovels for about one hour but found this method rather slow and difficult," he wrote. During that time, workers had been able to extricate only ten of the dead from what Fallon described as "the entangled mass of burned bodies . . .

piled from basement to six feet above floor under [the] stairs." In an attempt to speed up the gruesome process and keep from mutilating the bodies as much as possible, Fallon ordered that a stream of water be aimed under each body to loosen it from the charred mass, a technique that "proved satisfactory."

In his report issued later that day, Fallon resorted to an unfortunate and rather ugly simile to describe the results of the process: "The bodies floating around like beef in a vat." After removing 159 victims from the ruins, Fallon and his men searched to make sure no one had been left behind. He does not describe how they carried out this process. At the height of the fire, all three floors of the school had collapsed into the basement—a basement now filled with charred debris and flooded with water. In the coming days and weeks, Collinwood residents would reach the grim realization that the ashes of some of the victims most likely still lay scattered on the basement floor.

The outer shell of the burned-out building. Taken when the fire had been extinguished, the photograph shows the school's north side. (Courtesy of the Cleveland Public Library Photograph Collection)

Fallon notes in passing that the unpleasant recovery task was "hampered some on account of the parents of the dead children who were clamoring to get a glimpse of these little darlings as they were taken from ruins of the building to stretchers to ambulances." The line of ambulances and other conveyances moved slowly away from the smoking ruin south on Collamer to the temporary morgue. The ambulances and wagons repeated their melancholy journey until all of the extricated bodies had been delivered. Reportedly, many of the ambulance drivers—who were used to seeing sickness, death, and serious injury—finally broke down under the strain of endlessly repeating their grim odyssey. The *News* reported on March 5 that Julius Neibert, the father of Emma Neibert, who saw the first signs of the fire, was so grief-stricken over the death of two of his other children that he attacked an ambulance driver who refused to let him see the body he was transporting. Sometime around 5:00 P.M., Fallon and Collinwood mayor Westropp reviewed the situation and decided nothing more could be done on the scene; hence, as the gloom of night fell, the assembled masses of police, firemen, and onlookers drifted away from the still-smoldering ruin, surrendering it to silence and the descending darkness.

NOTES

It would seem that every research project invariably spawns a number of minor mysteries that stubbornly resist a solution. I can find no listing for the Hirter family in the 1900 Federal Census. The 1910 Census places them at the same address they occupied in 1908—447 Collamer; the Hirters still lived at this address in 1940. The 1910 form also enumerates the Hirter children not killed in the fire who were born in Ohio before 1900, but none of these names appear in the 1900 census. There are, however, two individuals identified only by the name "Harter" living at 171 Chestnut Street, the home of an accountant by the name of Robert Patterson. The form does not provide any other information, not even first names. In both cases, the note "not transcribed" appears after each of the Harter listings. Whether these two mysterious individuals, about whom nothing is known, are the elusive Fritz and Eliza Hirter is impossible to determine.

Edward Kern relates the stories of Alice Eichenberger and Angela Skerl in *The Collinwood School Fire of 1908* (11).

Kern quotes Pearl Lynn's testimony about dealing with her inability to control her students during the evacuation (*Collinwood School Fire,* 17). Unfortunately, he does not indicate the source. When and where did she make these remarks? She was excused from testifying from both the school board inquiry and the coroner's inquest due to the severity of her injuries.

Anna Moran's comments appeared in the March 6 edition of the *Press.* Judging by the date, the paper is most likely quoting her testimony from the coroner's inquest that morning. Lulu Rowley's words are taken from the article she supposedly wrote in the same issue of the afternoon daily.

Fritz Hirter's heartbreaking cry, "I had to leave my little child to die," has been quoted in a number of sources dealing with the fire. His desperate order to daughter Ella to run home is quoted in *Plain Dealer* writer Rachel Dissel's "Collinwood School Fire: 100 Years Later, an Angel Still Kneels over the Children" on March 2, 1908.

John Leffel's testimony is taken from Marshall Everett's *Complete Story of the Collinwood School Disaster and How Such Horrors Can Be Prevented,* as is Charles Wahl's (43, 44, 52). Everett typically does not identify his sources, but, since Leffel was called to appear at the coroner's inquest on March 9, it's probably safe to assume that Everett is quoting his inquest testimony. Wahl was not among those called to testify at the coroner's inquest; his comments, therefore, may have been made at the school board inquiry that commenced on the evening of March 4.

Kern quotes Joe Curran's anguished recollections (*Collinwood School Fire,* 36). Since Curran was not called to testify at the coroner's inquest, his testimony is most likely from the March 4 school board inquiry. Mrs. Walter C. Kelly's comments are quoted in Everett's *Collinwood School Fire* (62–64). Kelly was not called to testify at the coroner's inquest; hence, Everett is most likely repeating her testimony before the schoolboard. See Everett's work also for Wallace Upton's comment about the children's eyes and Harry Sigler's recollection (181, 188). Upton was called to testify before the coroner on March 9; Sigler was not.

One of the photographers on the scene was William Hubern Bullock, who actually filmed the catastrophe with a motion picture camera. Had it not been for Bullock, we would not have this brief record of the fire's aftermath and the subsequent burial of the unidentified at Lake View Cemetery. The short video fragment can be accessed online: "Collinwood School Fire," YouTube video, 3:05, posted by the Cleveland Public Library, February 16, 2008, https://www.youtube.com/watch?v=-KQU-DR9z2c.

The March 6 *Plain Dealer* carried the laudatory story of Chief Charles McIlrath's professionalism on the scene even as he remained ignorant of the ultimate fate of his own children.

Copies of Battalion Chief Michael A. Fallon's one-page typed report are contained in a multi-folder box of documents related to the Collinwood School Fire housed at the main branch of the Cleveland Public Library.

Chapter Four

DAYS OF SORROW
AND DESPAIR

He had wandered the muddy, partly frozen streets of Collinwood the entire night. John Oblak's daughter was still missing, hours after the devastating fire at Lakeview Elementary School had been extinguished and the last bodies had been conveyed to the temporary morgue. Deeply shocked and in a stupor, Oblak walked back and forth between the smoldering ruins of the school and the Lake Shore storehouse where the dead lay, on the off chance that he might find his child. He was not alone; dimly he recalled seeing the ghostly figures of distracted men and women also endlessly walking the dirty streets. He passed some of the silent wanderers several times during his lonely nocturnal odyssey. As the sun rose, Oblak—now cold and shivering—found himself standing on the front stoop of the house belonging to the pastor of his church—Father M. Pakis of St Mary's.

. . .

The agonizing events of the next few days would unfold at a much more deliberate pace than the hours of chaotic horror characterizing the fire; but the emotionally wrenching process of repeated recovery, identification, and burial would move grimly forward, generating extraordinary pain and unimaginable suffering in the neighborhood. Judging by the surviving photographs taken on the scene, it appears those working to remove the bodies of the dead from the smoking ruins carried them through the west doorway, where the terrible pileup

The grim process of removing the bodies of the dead through the western exit where most of the children died. Note that the interior of the building is still smoldering. (Everett, *Complete Story of the Collinwood School Disaster*)

Fire Marshal Harry T. Brockman questioning janitor Fritz Hirter in the immediate aftermath of the fire. Hirter lost three children in the disaster and sustained severe burns to his head and hands. The photograph clearly shows the bandages around his head. (Everett, *Complete Story of the Collinwood School Disaster*)

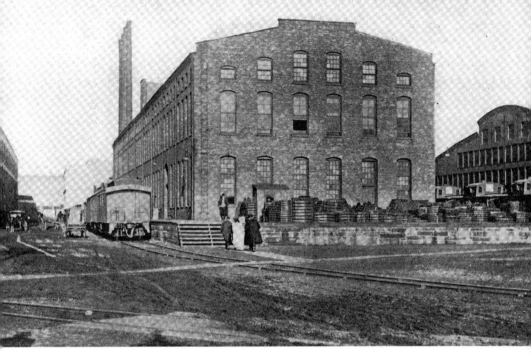

The Lake Shore Railroad storehouse that the company donated as a temporary morgue. (Everett, *Complete Story of the Collinwood School Disaster*)

of the doomed children had occurred. The calls went out for area ambulances to carry the dead to the storehouse, a desperate summons to which virtually every ambulance company in Cleveland responded.

Workers placed each body on a stretcher, covered it with a blanket, and carried it to an ambulance, wagon, or any other conveyance that had been pressed into service to transport the charred remains—the entire recovery effort constantly hampered by crowds of the morbidly curious. Hour after hour, well into the night, it went on—a seemingly endless, plodding parade of commandeered vehicles with their grim cargo. Lake Shore workers had cleared a space at the building donated by company officials to receive the staggeringly high number of burned corpses.

Many of the bodies had not survived the rigors of the extraction process intact; some were missing hands or limbs—others were missing heads. Some had been so badly damaged by the fire and the violence of the interior's collapse that only pieces and charred bones remained, and volunteers carried what they could gather to the morgue in baskets. Only a precious few could be identified through facial features; some were nothing more than masses of charred flesh and bone. Almost all were horribly contorted.

At the shop, the bodies were carefully laid out in rows of ten. When it was possible to tell the difference, boys and girls were placed in separate rows. Reportedly, heat still rose from the bodies—even in the cold interior of the warehouse—and mingled with the stench of burned flesh. Workers went through the pockets of the dead—assuming any part of their clothing had survived the fire—removing whatever trinkets and small treasures they found. Though some sources state that

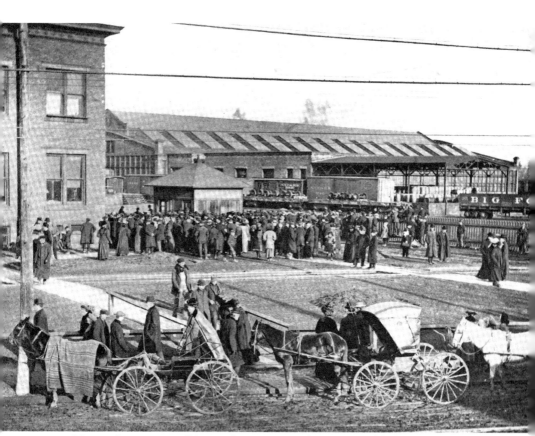

Distraught parents walking to the morgue. Volunteers would allow only ten in at a time. (Everett, *Complete Story of the Collinwood School Disaster*).

the recovered articles were placed on top of the blankets covering the corpses so distraught parents could identify their children without having to confront the horror of a charred and terribly mangled body, others insist volunteers placed the recovered items away from the bodies but were careful to note which article came from which corpse.

According to the *Press* on March 5, six of the surviving seven teachers fanned out through Collinwood—even as the remains were being transported—going from house to house with the same terrible question: "Are any of your children missing?" (Though she survived the fire, Pearl Lynn was too badly injured to participate.) Apparently, someone in authority deemed this canvasing of the entire neighborhood a necessary part of what would be an extraordinarily difficult identification process; in retrospect, however, such a demand seems rather insensitive, as the teachers must all have been numb with shock.

Some of the bereaved parents reacted kindly; others broke out in furious anger. "Never again will I let my boy go to school," shouted a grieving father who had lost his daughter. Bertha Robinson cried at Laura Bodey, "Why didn't you bring my little girls with you?" (The Robinson sisters—Fern, age twelve, and Wanita, age seven—were the only children of color at the school. Curiously, no contemporary source identified them as African American.) Constantly struggling to retain their composure, the devastated young women did their best to deal with all the softly muttered questions and the angrily shouted accusations.

There were, thankfully, occasional moments of joy to leaven the ordeal. "I'm so glad you threw me out the window," remarked one young girl to Lulu Rowley. "I only hurt my wrist." The mother of seven-year-old Bertha Jepson related how happy she was she had kept her daughter home due to illness. "I know she would have been killed because she isn't as strong as her comrades." As the teachers walked the streets, children who had escaped the burning building ran up to them with their exciting tales of good luck and grim accounts of their schoolmates who perished. They were also able to give the young women the names of those who had been trapped and had died. The teachers continued their inquiries until well into the night.

Though we remain painfully aware of the circumstances, we will never know how or who worked out the identification procedure. All that can be said is that someone with extraordinary management skills and enormous sensitivity established it quickly and efficiently and that those offering their services to the bereaved carried out their duties with as much care and compassion as possible. Cuyahoga County's Coroner Thomas A. Burke and his assistant, Deputy Coroner O'Neil, were there to oversee the operation. A temporary hospital with four nurses was also established on the building's second floor. Guards stood at the door and allowed the desperate parents into the yawning darkness of the cold space—now suffused with the sickening odor of charred flesh—ten at a time. Some sources allege that women were not allowed to enter the warehouse alone unless there were no men or teenage boys in the family to make the identification.

An escort led each person or couple into the forbidding space. Once inside, a volunteer accompanied the distraught parents as they slowly walked along the rows of covered corpses. The man in charge of the row would carefully lift the blanket from each body in succession so parents could look for something identifiable that had survived the fire—a piece of a coat or sweater, a shoe, a watch. The unimaginably grim ritual was repeated until every body had been checked. Once a body was identified, the blanket covering it would be removed and replaced with a white sheet and an attendant would check off that child's name from the list of pupils and attach a tag with his or her name to the sheet. The body then was sent either to the child's home for last rites or to the designated undertaker. To keep the intrusive crowds of gawkers away from the grieving parents, police cordoned off the building as well as possible. Initially, the morgue remained open for twenty-four hours. Some parents would return, searching, throughout the night. The morgue stayed open until all hope of anyone claiming the remaining corpses had passed; some of the bodies would never be identified.

Reporters representing all of Cleveland's newspapers moved through the mourning crowds as unobtrusively as possible, recording scores of heart-wrenching stories. It was an age that looked tolerantly,

The heart-wrenching scene in the Lake Shore storehouse as grieving parents try to identify the bodies of their children. The blanket-covered corpses were lined up in rows of ten. The photograph lends support to the assertion that women were not permitted to enter the temporary morgue alone unless there was no male family alternative. (Everett, *Complete Story of the Collinwood School Disaster*).

even kindly, on a woman's dramatic show of hysteria under extreme duress. Cries of anguish were common; many mothers simply fainted. Some of the fathers broke down weeping under the emotional strain; others remained almost defiantly stoic. One father was so badly shaken he had to be supported by two attendants to keep him from collapsing as he moved from one body to the next. One distraught woman repeatedly screamed, "Oh, Henry. Henry," as she gazed at each body in turn in her desperate quest to locate her son. In a heartrending display of grief she reportedly clawed at the burned and torn remnants of clothing that clung to each corpse. "That's Henry's sweater," she moaned as she knelt over one of the bodies. When escorts tried to lead her from the building, she resisted. "That's only one," she whispered and walked on. Newspapers later identified the subject of the poor woman's desperate search as Henry Schultz. The nine-year-old boy remains the only Schultz to have died in the fire; hence his mother, thankfully, did not lose any other children.

Hour after hour, the ghostly figures of emotionally drained parents drifted slowly through the cold darkness—up one row, down the next—the painful silence broken by either gentle sobbing or hysterical cries. It was an agonizingly slow process. As attendants led him out of the warehouse, one father sobbed, "Oh, God, let me go too. Why did I live to see this day?" Finally, one woman knelt over a body, lifted a glistening suspender buckle from a charred mass of cloth, and kissed it. Nils Thompson! The first identification had been made. One man wandered up and down the rows of dark forms holding a young girl by the hand, his face resolutely turned away from the appalling sights. "This is Irene's skirt, daddy," she murmured after an unbearably long search. Irene Davis! Another identification had been made.

Wednesday had been thirteen-year-old Don Rush's birthday. His father identified his son's body from the charm he had given him as a present. "I could tell my boy's coat," sobbed one woman. "It was a little plaid coat." Another grieving mother thought she could recognize her son by his new red sweater with braid on the front. Eight-year-old Dale Clark was identified by a pink-bordered handkerchief in which he had wrapped a green marble. John Newsberry recognized his son Russell from a small watch chain. Marija Drescik was identified through an earring. "No, no, these are not George's buttons," moaned Mrs. John Centener as she examined a shred of underwear still stuck to one of the bodies. "If there was only a piece of his red sweater, I could tell him." One woman identified her son by the silver watch that had belonged to her late husband.

Eleven-year-old Albert Gould's sister recognized her brother's shoes and sweater; his cousin Raymond Gould was identified through his shirt-cuff button. John Polomsky identified his son Victor from a piece of cloth on one of the boy's shriveled arms; the boy's shirt had been made from the same material as his mother's apron. "Look carefully now," an escort gently counseled a distracted woman who scanned the rows of shrouded bodies, utterly at a loss. One woman silently walked up and down the rows of bodies accompanied by her husband, her face frozen in a stoic mask; with no trace of emotion, she identified her child and left instructions for the undertaker. Once outside, however, she lost all control and fainted. An elderly Polish woman brushed away attendants when they tried to offer support. "Leave me alone," she commanded. "Do you think I would not know my boy?" Another woman came to the temporary morgue every day; she stood at the foot of the same body and wept, refusing to admit the child was hers.

A grandfather dropped to his knees and kissed the feet of his granddaughter, whom he had finally recognized through her shoes. Another man identified his son through a list of spelling words in the boy's pocket, which had miraculously survived the fire. Though newspaperman Walter C. Kelly and his wife managed to identify the body of son Walter Jr., the corpse of their younger son, Richard Dewey, initially eluded them. "If I could but know that what is left of my boy was in my own hands," moaned one distraught mother. "I can't bear to leave his body if it is here. I must find it, must find it."

The intrusive and insensitive phenomenon known today as ambulance-chasing is, unfortunately, not new; it showed its ugly face repeatedly at that warehouse morgue. Some of the solicitors representing local undertaking establishments shoved business cards at the grieving parents so aggressively that volunteers who shepherded the distraught families through the identification process had to warn them off.

The reporters who staked out both the smoking ruins of the school and the temporary morgue kept track of the disaster's appalling statistics: how many dead, identified, and yet to be identified. The city's major dailies passed the grim numbers on to their readers and constantly updated them—almost on an hour-by-hour basis. On March 4, the *Press* put the death toll at "fully one hundred." The *News* initially specified 146 and upped the total to "nearly" 150 the next day, then settled on 161 in a later edition. On March 5, the *Press* confidently proclaimed that by two o'clock that afternoon 131 victims had been positively identified. The same day, the *Plain Dealer* maintained that 165 children had lost their lives; on March 7 it put the final death toll at 174: 172 children and 2 teachers.

Considering the physical condition of the bodies and the circumstances at the temporary morgue, the identification process moved along remarkably quickly. By 4:00 P.M. on March 5, the *Plain Dealer* could report that more than half of the bodies at the Lake Shore building had been identified. On the same day, the *News* said that 139 had been positively identified. The same day, the *Press* maintained that 28 awaited identification; by March 7, the *Plain Dealer* put the number of unidentified at 21—a group the paper described on March 6 as representing "the survival of the unfittest"—a clear reference to the deplorable condition of the bodies. On Monday, March 9, the *News* reported that two more bodies had been identified, putting the final total of the unclaimed at 19.

The major city dailies also ran lists of the dead and missing, all replete with the spelling mistakes and first name inaccuracies that would cripple attempts to arrive at a definite accounting of the victims for over a century. Unfortunately, it is possible, even likely, that some of those claimed and buried may not have been positively identified. On March 5, the *News* informed readers, "If any family that has lost a child and cannot find the boy or girl should wish to bury one of the unrecognizable bodies, they will be permitted to do so." The Ritzi family had lost daughters Clara and Helen; the Grants lost daughter Earla. Their bodies were never identified. There is no record of how many grieving families may have responded to this generous and undoubtedly heartfelt offer, but it would obviously seriously complicate the identification process, not only then, but for years to come.

Given the terrible condition of the bodies and the horrendous circumstances under which traumatized parents were forced to make identifications, it was inevitable that mistakes would be made and fights break out over who had the rights to a given corpse. On March 7, a headline in the *Press* proclaimed, "Parents Bury Wrong Bodies." John Leibritzer came to the morgue on Saturday looking for the body of his son Ferdinand, which he had identified the day before. "I identified my boy by his clothing and shoes," the outraged father maintained. "A tag was placed on his body and an undertaker was given orders to take charge of the remains." But the remains never arrived at the family home on Oak Street. "I have not seen the body since Friday night and no one seems to know anything about my boy's remains." John Zimmerman and James Lowry both claimed the body of a little girl who had died in Glenville Hospital a few hours after the fire. Deputy Coroner O'Neil halted burial until he could make a reasonably positive identification.

H. Zingelman and Otto Markushatt fought over the same body, the former insisting it was his eight-year-old son Harry and the later stoutly maintaining it was his thirteen-year-old son Elmer. Services for Harry and his sister Lucy had been completed at the Zingelman home, and the family was actually in the process of burying their children in Lake View Cemetery when Deputy Coroner O'Neil intervened and took charge of the corpse, explaining it would be kept in a vault until he could make a thorough investigation. On March 6, the *News* carried the poignant story of the little neighborhood girl who timidly came to the Zingelman residence with a handful of nickels and pennies. She went up to first woman she saw and, with lips trembling, whispered, "Give them to Lucy's ma. I'm so sorry and want to help."

Markushatt immediately became embroiled in a second dispute, fighting with Harry W. Sigler over the identification of a body each man steadfastly maintained was his daughter. "She was my girl Mabel," insisted Sigler to the *Plain Dealer*. "I recognized her body by her hair." "He's wrong," countered Markushatt. "She was my Elsie; I would recognize her hair among a thousand." The odyssey of the disputed body is unfortunately lost in the understandable chaos that reigned during and after the fire. Somehow, the girl's remains initially were taken to a facility that the *Plain Dealer* identified as the "Hogan & Co.'s Glenville morgue." From there, the body went to the temporary morgue, where both men claimed it. In this case, O'Neil did not intervene, and the body was ultimately buried as Mabel Sigler. Since he was busy with funeral arrangements for his son Elmer, Markushatt didn't object; apparently, his dispute with H. Zingleman was ultimately resolved in Markushatt's favor.

The terrible death of their son Emil couldn't mend relations, however momentarily, between a divorced father and mother. Both L. W. Rostock and his ex-wife, Effie, claimed the body of their six-year-old son. The mother had obtained sole custody at the time of the divorce and had since remarried. The boy's stepfather, Clinton Taylor, identified the body, but Rostock asserted that, as the child's father, he should be in charge of John's final disposition. The wrangling grew to such a fevered pitch that O'Neil ordered a police officer to guard the body until the court could intervene.

"We have been exceedingly careful with the bodies," O'Neil assured the *Press* on March 7. "It would be impossible to prevent mistakes, however, especially where parents visited the morgue and stated positively that the body before them as that of a lost child." (O'Neil does not mention the poor condition of the bodies as a contributing factor in the identification process.) "Everything will be done to make the identification of bodies complete." Though city papers obviously found these ugly conflicts in the midst of tragedy eminently newsworthy, they took little interest in reporting how any of them were resolved.

. . .

At the close of March 4, volunteers transported the unidentified bodies to an apparently vacant fire shed adjacent the town hall. No reason was ever provided for the action, but it may have had something to do with easing the congestion at the storehouse and facilitating the delivery of identified remains to either family homes or undertakers. Somehow the intrusive crowds that had milled around the school as it burned the day before, hindering both rescue and recovery efforts, learned of the transfer and showed up in force on the morning of March 5.

"Vulturelike, the Curious Gaze at Saddened Souls Laid Bare," proclaimed the *Plain Dealer* on March 6. Reporters from the same newspaper watched in total disgust as a huge crowd "congested the street" and "pressed against the police cordon which surrounded the Collinwood town hall." In something akin to stunned disbelief, the paper indignantly observed, "The crowd was added to as the cars came in from the city loaded to the running boards." Of Cleveland's largest papers, the *Plain Dealer* clearly seemed angered the most by what the reporters saw as the massive insensitive intrusion of large crowds all through

Collinwood during the fire and its aftermath. (Judging by its coverage, the *Press* showed little interest in such bothersome side issues.)

The men from the *Plain Dealer* wandered through the crowds, picking up and recording stray comments that floated through the air. "If I had my way, I wouldn't rest until the fellow responsible for this was in jail," proclaimed one observer to no one in particular. "What I want to know," volunteered another, "is where is the janitor?" "No fault of his," remarked a third man. "The doors opened inward—that's how it happened." (Thus the myth of the inward-swinging doors was born!) The crowd milled around for most of the day, until an unidentified man rushed from the town hall shouting, "Fire!" The *Plain Dealer* wryly noted that the mob had "a new and different diversion" with which to occupy itself. When it turned out to be a false alarm, the paper observed with disgust, "The crowd was amused. A false alarm is always amusing."

. . .

The response to the Collinwood disaster from every local quarter was exemplary: the shopmen from Lake Shore, neighborhood residents, the Salvation Army, and other official and unofficial agencies from all over greater Cleveland all rushed to the scene of the fire and fanned out into the neighborhood to offer what assistance and comfort they could. "There is no dressing of wounds to be done," remarked a physician identified only as Dr. C. S. Anderson to the *Plain Dealer* on March 6. "The children are all dead, but there are prostrated families by the score where the presence of a trained nurse is of the greatest value." Accordingly, Huron Road Hospital sent a contingent of nurses to Collinwood, and Mary Johnson, superintendent of the Visiting Nurses' Association, dispatched twenty well-trained volunteer nurses.

At a board meeting of the VNA on April 1, Johnson reported that the nurses had made a total of 3,108 calls in the neighborhood and treated 580 patients. They found mothers so distraught over the losses of children that they were unable to function. "Though there was little to be done for the injured children, there was much for a Nurse to do in the stricken households, for in many cases the Mothers were entirely prostrated by grief and needed intelligent care. And in some cases the shock was so great that they have not yet recovered." The local chapter of the YWCA contributed a hundred volunteers to help care for the injured and aid in making funeral arrangements.

Collinwood mayor Westropp appointed a nine-man support committee, drawn from members of the board of trade. Headquartered in a store on Collamer opposite the town hall, the committee would organize and spearhead all neighborhood relief activities. "All cases of destitution were reported there and immediate relief sent to the afflicted families," the *Plain Dealer* assured its readers. "A house to house canvas was made of the entire town and any case noted where help was needed. Money and coal were provided to thirty families, mostly in the Greiner [poor German and Slovenian] district." On March 6, the *News* enumerated the needs volunteers would try to meet: medical, food, clothing, fuel, nursing, and "women's care." The paper also reported that local clothing manufactures and stores were donating black suits and any other articles of attire to the poorest families of the neighborhood so they would have something appropriate to wear as they honored both their dead children and their church at the funerals.

On March 6, the *Plain Dealer* carried a plea from Frank P. Whitney, superintendent of schools: "Brave Women Wanted to Serve Homes and Mete Out Care." Whitney maintained that these volunteers should be prepared to take charge of bereaved households and stay for perhaps two or three days. "We need women who know the duties of mothers; women who can go into our stricken homes and relieve the burdened, grief stricken women here of the care of their families," he told a committee of Lake Shore superintendents and foremen. If there were any awards to be handed out for the speed, depth, and effectiveness of the responses to this call for help, they would unquestionably be given to the neighborhood churches and county religious organizations.

Reverend C. Parker, pastor of the local Congregational church, joined with Marie Reitinger, representing Associated Charities, in visiting every family in the area deemed destitute; Reverend M. L. Beckley, pastor of the Collinwood Church of Christ, canvased every family in the territory served by his church. Father M. Pakis officiated as priest at St. Mary's in what the *Plain Dealer* referred to as the "Greiner parish," probably the poorest section of Collinwood. Church members—many of whom had been out of work for months and did not speak English—gathered in Father Pakis's study to grieve and share their losses with neighbors. The priest thought as many as thirty of the children in his parish were either dead or among the missing. The Christian Endeavor Union of Cuyahoga County responded to appeals by sending two hundred female volunteers into the village to work with the committees and local ministers. They offered to provide music for funeral services and mourning clothes for destitute families. "We do not believe in praying and doing nothing else," declared Mrs. McWilliams, wife of one of the pastors of Calvary Presbyterian Church, to the *Plain Dealer* on March 6. "We are giving too. Calvary Church is back of every stricken family in its parish." Her husband, Dr. T. S. McWilliams, teamed up with Reverend E. R. Wright to visit every afflicted family in the congregation of the main church at Euclid Avenue and East Seventy-Ninth Street, and its offshoot on Collamer Avenue. The church had lost somewhere between thirty-seven and forty children, fully one-third of its Sunday school class.

The women of the Christian Endeavor Union who spread out through Collinwood's poorer neighborhoods with the nurses and other volunteers not only confronted insurmountable language barriers but most likely faced a level of poverty and a depth of grief that left them badly shaken. Individuals whom the press simply described as "committee members" knocked on the door at 4811 Charles Street but received no answer. When they pushed open the unlocked door and peered into a cold, virtually empty room, they were greeted by a disheveled, frantic woman holding a knife to her own throat, identified by the *Plain Dealer* only as Mrs. Maknic. The would-be comforters caught the name *Mary* and the word *missing* while the men in the group wrestled the knife from the distraught woman as she muttered incoherently in a language no one understood. The committee members found neither food nor warming fire at the home of Mary Popovic. Rather, they encountered a woman huddled in a rocking chair and wrapped in a ragged shawl, glaring at them with bloodshot eyes. Though the

Plain Dealer intimated that the poor woman had lost two children, the only Popovic on the list of victims is John Popovic.

There seemed no end to the heartbreaking stories of grief and loss throughout Collinwood. "Everywhere within a radius of a half mile is misery, hopelessness and the gloom of death," wrote *Press* reporter Dorothy Dale. "Of all the death mown thoroughfares in Collinwood, Arcade St. is the most desolate," the paper proclaimed in a separate article. Houses in which a dead or missing child had lived were marked with a white ribbon. Cleveland's four major dailies presented the sad stories they cataloged as if the reporter had been an eyewitness. Obviously, it would have been impossible for the reporters to be in so many places at precisely the right moment. No doubt, in some cases they were repeating stories relayed to them by those volunteers who methodically visited house after house.

A woman whom the *Press* identified as Mrs. H. W. Zeigler of Arcade Street wept as she desperately held on to the belief that her only child, daughter Mabel, was just missing temporarily and was not among those who died. All hopes were dashed when her husband entered the house and sadly announced he had located her body at the morgue. Mrs. W. H. Walden had not been told that her daughter Luella had died in the fire because, according to the *Press,* the poor woman lay near death, though her illness was not specified. When she asked why Luella had not come home Wednesday evening, family members told her that her daughter was staying with neighbors. The *Press* described an unidentified man sitting at his kitchen table, staring at nothing, while his wife knelt and sobbed by the bodies of dead children in the front room. In another home, a baby in its high chair pounded the tray in front petulantly with a spoon while demanding to know when Alice was coming home. (This was probably a reference to Mary Alice Burrows, the only "Alice" among those who died.)

Convinced that her ten-year-old son, Allen, had survived the disaster, Mrs. Mary Hinsdale wandered the streets of Collinwood distractedly for several days looking for him. "Many people have told me that Allen jumped from the window," the desperate woman told the *Plain Dealer* on March 8. She even petitioned school superintendent Frank Whitney to

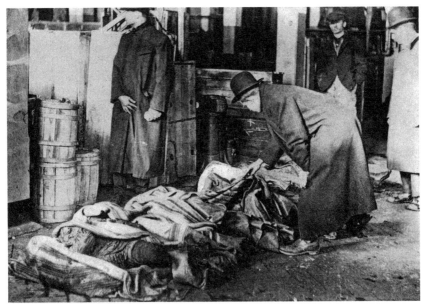

The painful identification process. (Everett, *Complete Story of the Collinwood School Disaster*)

send out a search party, believing that some kind neighbors had taken her son into their home but that because of his injuries, the boy could not tell anyone his name. Her friends lamented that the poor woman had come unhinged and would always believe Allen was alive, though he had already been numbered among the dead.

Janitor Fritz Hirter's son Walter was among the first to get out of the building, but he returned in search of his sister Ida. Neither survived. Margaret Caravona's mother broke down completely when she learned of her only daughter's death. According to the *Press,* the hysterical woman tore her hair while screaming loudly; reportedly her agonized cries could be heard for blocks. In a vain attempt to locate the body of his fourteen-year-old daughter, Hattie, Harry Marks came to the storehouse-turned-morgue several times on Wednesday. The girl had not been seen since the disaster, and Marks assumed she had been among the fire's victims. On Thursday morning, he returned to the morgue one last time, only to see Hattie standing in the crowd surrounding the building. Wednesday morning, instead of going to school, she had run off to visit her aunt in Cleveland and had not heard of the fire until Thursday morning. Early Saturday morning, March 7, eleven-year-old Glen Barber died in Glenville Hospital, thus becoming the last of the 172 Lakeview students to lose his life. Between bouts of delirium, suffering from bad burns and internal injuries sustained in his jump from a second-story window, the boy spoke of his escape. The day after his death, the *Plain Dealer* recounted his last words: "I am standing on a large rock, larger than all the world."

. . .

Of the nine teachers at Lakeview Elementary, six escaped the disaster physically unscathed. First-grade teacher Pearl Lynn sustained severe burns to her back before rescuers Frank Dorn and Charles Wahl could pull her, virtually unconscious, to safety through the rear door, her clothes badly burned and torn. The poor woman became hysterical Thursday night, and by Friday she had fallen into a state of virtual mental collapse—a condition that would excuse her from testifying at the coroner's inquest on Friday, March 6.

Third-grade teacher Grace Fiske tried to control the crush of panicked children rushing toward the rear doors but was trampled by the very students she was trying to save. Would-be rescuer Max Shubert of Lake Avenue witnessed her frantic struggles but couldn't help her. "She was jammed so tight against it [the rear door] she couldn't move," he told the *Press*. "She was half in and half out. I tried to pull her out. I tried to pull children out, but they were wedged so tightly I couldn't." When rescuers finally located and uncovered her, they found the charred remains of two children wrapped in her skirts. Though Grace Fiske survived the fire, she died around noon at Glenville Hospital.

The last time anyone saw second-grade teacher Katherine Weiler, she was frantically attempting to redirect children away from the clogged rear door to the fire escape on the second floor, even as her own clothes were burning. "Teacher Chooses Death That Others May Live," proclaimed the *Plain Dealer*. Like Grace Fiske, she fell before the surging, unstoppable wave of frightened students stampeding toward the rear doors just as the building's three floors collapsed into the base-

Left: Third-grade teacher Grace Fiske. Although she initially survived the fire, she succumbed to her injuries later that afternoon at Glenville Hospital. When rescuers pulled her from the burning building, they found the bodies of two dead children wrapped in her skirt. (Everett, *Complete Story of the Collinwood School Disaster*). *Right:* Second-grade teacher Katherine Weiler. Deeply devoted to her students, she died trying to steer them toward the building's sole fire escape. Her body was never recovered. (Everett, *Complete Story of the Collinwood School Disaster*)

ment, accompanied by a thunderous crash and a huge roiling cloud of smoke and flames. Katherine's father, the Reverend Gustav Weiler of Pittsburgh, was making a "pastoral call" when the telegram from Superintendent Frank P. Whitney arrived at his home around 3:30 P.M. "Daughter burnt in Lakeview school building fire this morning." A second telegram, from Katherine's landlord, Frank W. Lindow, arrived about an hour later. "Come to Cleveland at once. Katherine is dead." In his memorial tribute to his daughter, the Reverend Weiler wrote of "the terrible duty of seeking for her remains among the charred, distorted and disremembered corpses, the awful, awful fruit of the fire." At nearly six feet in height, Katherine was a commanding presence in the classroom, towering above her students. She was extraordinarily tall for a woman in the early years of the twentieth century; given her stature, it's logical to assume that her remains would clearly stand out among the much smaller bodies of the students. Searchers discovered a larger body in a tangled mass of smaller ones around 1:00 P.M. the day of the fire, and newspapers speculated that it could be the missing teacher. On March 5, the *Plain Dealer* assured its readers that Miss Weiler's corpse had, indeed, been recovered: "Her mangled body was pulled out of the smoking ruins by nightfall."

Katherine's father came to Cleveland from his Pittsburgh home, joining her younger brothers William and Henry from Canton, and spent two agonizing days walking silently and sadly back and forth between the rows of covered corpses in a vain attempt to identify her body. For reasons never clarified, William carried one of her shoes with him. The Weilers also came armed with a description of her dental work. By Thursday night, they had made a tentative identification. Dr. E. Hill of Collamer Street pried open the mouth of the corpse thought to be Katherine and compared the teeth with the description he had been given. He looked up and affirmed, "It is she." "The dental work corresponds perfectly with the description furnished me," Hill assured the *News*. "Remains found," Reverend Weiler wired his wife. "Funeral Saturday 2 P.M. Come on 5 o'clock Penna, train." The body then was turned over to a local undertaker.

By Friday afternoon, however, Dr. D. H. Patterson had dismissed Dr. Hill's identification, since his closer examination of the remains revealed them to be male. Ultimately, the body was identified as that of John Kranjnak of Hale Street, a would-be rescuer whom onlookers remembered having seen running into the burning building. Officials based the identification on the simple fact that Kranjnak had not been seen since the fire. Disheartened and deeply disappointed, Reverend Weiler wired his wife at 4:30. "Mistake has been made. Remains found are not Katherine's. Do not come." Her father and two brothers returned to the temporary morgue early Friday evening. Katherine Weiler's body, however, seems to have vanished. "We have not been able to discover the body in the ruins or at any of the morgues," Gustav Weiler told the *Plain Dealer* on March 6. "I have almost lost hope of ever being able to find her." Yet Barney Reiche of Foster Avenue insisted her body had to be somewhere. "I myself took Miss Weiler's body from the building," he insisted to the *Press* on Saturday, March 7, "and placed it on a stretcher. I am certain it is not among the unidentified bodies." Reiche would certainly be able to tell whether the body he placed on the stretcher was a child or an adult. No one in the press, however, followed up on his claim. The body of Katherine Weiler was never recovered.

"The last hope had vanished," wrote her father in his memorial tribute. It is possible that the fire's incredible heat totally incinerated her body, or perhaps it simply did not survive intact the collapse of the three floors into the basement or the rigors of the extrication process. Reverend Weiler lamented that circumstances had deprived his family of a grave at which they could mourn. Most likely, Katherine Weiler's remains still rest among the scattered unrecovered ashes of her students beneath the memorial garden that today stands over the spot where most of the children died.

Like a small, lone flower blossoming in the midst of a blasted landscape, however, at least one story of hope and renewal emerged from among all the heart-wrenching details: Katherine Weiler's thirty-one-year-old brother William found a wife. He had formerly been engaged to Norma Frau, a twenty-two-year old nurse. The engagement had been broken off sometime in 1906, and the couple had not seen each other since. Almost miraculously, William encountered Norma as, deeply discouraged, he wandered the streets of Collinwood during the days his family searched unsuccessfully for Katherine's body. The meeting resulted in a reconciliation and a renewed engagement. The pair married in Norma Frau's home on Carnegie on June 16, 1908.

· · ·

Though newspaper stories tended to emphasize the depth of loss and the emotional devastation in Collinwood—at least initially, they also focused on some urgent practical matters demanding immediate attention. How could a relatively small community with a finite number of churches hold services for 172 children? How could that same community handle the burial of so many within a few days? How could the poorer families of that neighborhood pay for a simple casket and the other trappings of a proper funeral? In today's world of instantaneous communication and the rapid dissemination of news, major disasters can be met quickly with a televised fundraiser featuring the nation's top musical performers, all of whom donate their services. In the early years of the twentieth century, news of tragic events and the public response to them moved far more slowly, but the nature of the response from both private and public entities was remarkably similar.

On Thursday, March 5, the *Press* announced that H. F. Keith, owner of the Keith Theater at East 105th Street and Euclid Avenue, ordered the facility's manager to arrange a benefit performance of traditional vaudeville acts to help raise money. World-famous escape artist Harry Houdini topped the bill, along with noted American actress Blanche Bates. All the performers donated their services. There would be no admission charge, though theater management placed a box in the lobby to receive "whatever gifts of money" patrons cared to donate. The event raised $285.05.

Both the *News* and the *Plain Dealer* established relief funds. (Instead of raising money, the *Press* opted to do an in-depth study of school safety in Cleveland.) By Friday, March 6, the *News* could boast of having raised $1,673.23. By the evening of March 5, the city's morning paper the *Plain Dealer* announced that more than $1,000 had been raised; and by the next day, the daily could proudly maintain that their fund had reached the $2,500 mark. Money also poured in from private donors all over the county and from employees from city businesses and industries, such as the Ology Cigar factory, the Standard Welding Co., and the Zipp Manufacturing Co. The Collinwood Board of Trade and the city council donated $5,000 each. The Ohio State legislature voted unanimously to contribute $25,000. All donations passed through the hands of Collinwood Relief Committee treasurer F. H. Houghton. The final total of all donated funds reached $50,000—worth well over $1.2 million today.

Ohio governor Andrew L. Harris appointed Collinwood mayor Westropp and Cleveland mayor Tom L. Johnson to head a committee to oversee the distribution of funds. The organization divided Collinwood into eight districts and then within those districts distributed money to be used primarily for funeral expenses, food, and coal. Regrettably, the tragedy brought out the worst in people as well as the best. On March 7, the *Press* warned city residents to be wary of lone individuals soliciting money: "Any person representing himself or herself as a *Press* solicitor of funds for Collinwood is an imposter. If you are solicited, notify the police. A fraudulent woman solicitor was working in Woodland Avenue Saturday afternoon."

· · ·

The funerals began in the devastated community before midnight on Thursday evening, March 5, when James, Norman, and Maxwell Turner were buried after services conducted at the family home by Rev. Gerard F. Patterson of St. Stephen's Episcopal Mission.

All of Cleveland—indeed, all of Cuyahoga County—watched as Collinwood solemnly buried an entire generation. Many of the services to follow were private affairs, carried out in family homes. Some local churches held mass services for all the children in their congregations; some buried their dead individually, although it is not clear if that meant individual services or individual burials. City newspapers remain the only window we have on those solemn days, and reporters obviously couldn't be everywhere. What survives is a collection of snapshots and fragments—pieces of an incomplete puzzle. Large funeral processions and mass church services received most of the attention—although reporters often followed up on services for children who had been identified by name and whose individual stories appeared in the coverage of the fire itself.

Cuyahoga County's Sheriff McGorry had worried that trouble could break out if saloons remained open during the week of mourning because grieving fathers might overwhelm local saloons "and get to drinking." Doubting he had the authority to order a neighborhood-wide shutdown and fully aware that he would be asking establishment proprietors to forgo at least a couple day's revenue, Mayor Westropp personally visited all the local saloons and asked them to close voluntarily.

Eleven-year-old Alma Gilbert had been one of the first of the dead recovered from the ruins of the school and among the very first identified at the Lake Shore storehouse. According to the *News* on March 5, her funeral was one of those that marked the beginning of nearly a week of solemn official services. Rites for fourteen-year-old Morris Sheppard immediately followed. Reverend E. R. Wright, pastor of Calvary Presbyterian Church, held his first funeral service, for thirteen-year-old Esther Hummel, at 5:30 A.M. on Friday, March 6. The church had lost perhaps as many as forty children from its Sunday school class, and Wright took charge in arranging a service in each home.

On the morning of Saturday, March 7, the *Plain Dealer* reported that there had been at least forty funerals the day before, an average of four an hour. There had been a double funeral for eleven-year-old cousins Albert and Raymond Gould at three o'clock in the afternoon and a second one an hour later for Sanderson brothers Glen, age twelve, and Harold, age nine. Of necessity, most of these services were abbreviated; and minsters exhausted themselves by spending entire days, from dawn to dusk, going from house to house. Unable to cover funeral expenses on their own, some of the poorer immigrant families assumed no financial help would be forthcoming, since many of them were not yet naturalized. When necessary, however, the village covered costs with money from the relief fund.

In the late afternoon of Friday, March 6, the *News* provided readers with a heart-wrenching description of white hearses moving slowly down virtually every street in Collinwood. Heads bowed, the grieving parents rode in carriages behind the hearses. "Scarcely did one funeral carriage pass before another came into sight wending its way with its sorrowful burden to the burying grounds," reported the *Press* on March 7. "Through the main street of the town the funeral[s] passed all day in one continuous procession." "The hearses marked where one funeral cortege ended and the next began. The horse[s] were kept trotting. Only at this pace could all be gotten to the cemetery."

In the village's ethnic enclaves, mourners honored their new homeland even as they embraced their old-world traditions. St. Mary's Slovenian Catholic Church looked after the spiritual needs in one of

Collinwood's poorer neighborhoods—a Greiner district where few spoke English and jobs were scarce. The parish had lost sixteen children. A huge American flag was draped above the main entrance of the church. A procession of young girls carrying large candles, followed by pallbearers with sixteen white caskets adorned with white flowers, filed slowly into the church, accompanied by the deep tolling of the large bell in the tower and followed by the mourning parents. Neighborhood children—including some who had survived the fire—served as pallbearers. Members of various societies, holding American flags and the emblems of their social organizations, lined the street as the solemn procession passed: the St. Vitus Society, the Slovenian Lodge, the League of the Sacred Heart, and the Confraternity of St. Barbara. Four rows of pews had been removed from the front of the church so that all sixteen caskets could be lined up at the foot of the altar rail. As the hushed, solemn chanting of the requiem mass ceased, muted sobs accompanied Father Pakis as he walked slowly by the row of caskets and blessed each one.

St. Joseph's Catholic Church held a similar service on Saturday for the twelve parish children lost in the disaster. Two of the mothers broke down in hysterics and fainted during the service and had to be taken out of the church to recover. All twelve children were buried in one wide grave at Euclid Catholic Cemetery. Services at Grace Lutheran Sunday School followed the next day. On March 6, every Cleveland school held a memorial service for the fire's victims.

The question of the disposition of the unidentified bodies had loomed large from the moment shocked and grieving parents first entered the temporary morgue to claim their dead. There were bodies burned beyond recognition or otherwise so badly damaged that identification was simply not possible. Some distraught parents had come to the Lake Shore storehouse repeatedly to confront the remaining charred masses, hoping against hope that something previously missed would help them identify their child. In a remarkable display of personal strength and sensitivity, John Woodhouse, father of missing Edgar Woodhouse, suggested that the ashes that might contain human remains should be scooped from the basement of the

The scene early morning of Monday, March 9, at Lake View Cemetery, preparations for the mass funeral of the unidentified. (Courtesy of the Cleveland Public Library Photograph Collection)

destroyed building and buried together with the unidentified. "Those ashes in the building are sacred to those of us who have been unable to identify our lost ones," Woodhouse told the *News*.

By Monday morning, the total of the unclaimed stood at twenty-one. According to some sources, Collinwood officialdom decided to forgo formal church services and simply bury the bodies at Lake View Cemetery. (Yet, on March 9 the *News* referred to "brief funeral services" before the unidentified were interred.) The Collinwood city council began to worry that the unidentified bodies still stored in the town hall were becoming a threat to public health; therefore, the council authorized the money from the relief fund to pay for the plots at Lake View Cemetery, as well as the small white caskets.

At literally the last minute on Monday morning, two final identifications were made—one of them Edgar, the son of John Woodhouse—reducing the number of unknowns to nineteen. Twelve funeral cars stood in a line on what the *News* simply called "the main street of the village." The families who finally had given up hope of identifying the bodies of their children watched quietly as pall bearers placed the nineteen caskets—any one of which might contain the remains of their loved one—into the two waiting funeral cars. The ten cars that followed had been reserved especially for them. A carload of flowers donated by Cleveland and Collinwood schoolchildren preceded the arrival of the funeral cortege at the cemetery. Flowers lined the graves, adorned the caskets, and provided a bed on which the caskets rested before burial. Thousands gathered at Lake View Cemetery to attend the service that included prayers in English and German; a short address by Miss Eva Booth, commander of the Salvation Army; as well as hymns sung by a choir of forty young women from area colleges. William Hubern Bullock caught slightly over a minute of the proceedings on motion picture. The camera first pans from right to left to show the sheer size of the massive crowd, then cuts to the workers digging the individual graves—little more than a scratched and blurred window looking out on another age; it is invaluable.

. . .

By Tuesday evening, March 10, the Herculean task of burying 172 children, both identified and unidentified, came to an end. The school ruins had cooled sufficiently to allow building inspectors to study the full extent of the damage, search for the fire's yet-to-be-determined cause, and assess the strength of the still-standing outer walls. In the days following the funerals, workers returned to the burned-out site one last time to clear the ashes from the basement. They sifted carefully through the charred debris to make sure no human remains were left behind. They uncovered a chunk of gold—most likely what was left of a child's watch. Surely, however, the completely incinerated remains of some of the children lay mixed with the structural debris. There was certainly no way to distinguish human ashes from those of the school's wooden interior; there is no record of what became of the material workers removed from the basement on their last trip to the melancholy site.

Though the public side of the story had ended, the tale of the Collinwood School Fire was hardly over. Grief would continue unabated and unobserved behind closed doors; some residents who lost children reported hearing them murmuring softly in dark rooms and corners of family homes. After a few weeks had passed, the ghostly whispers ceased. Some families simply left the neighborhood. The official search for the cause of the worst school fire in American history moved forward. There had to be a reason. There had to be an explanation. Surely, someone bore responsibility.

NOTES

The poignant story of John Oblak provides a snapshot of the overwhelming grief and despair suffered by the Collinwood parents who had either lost a child in the catastrophe or—far worse—did not know their children's ultimate fates. The report, which appeared in the *Plain Dealer* on March 6, also demonstrates the problems a researcher encounters when the only primary sources available are newspaper articles. The paper incorrectly identified John Oblak as John Oblock. The daughter for whom he searched was not identified by name. The only Oblak, however, on the list of victims is thirteen-year-old "John Oblak"—obviously Oblak's son.

The 1910 Federal Census lists Mary, a twelve-year-old daughter, as the only child in the Oblak household—no doubt the daughter for whom Oblak searched that night. She would have been ten in 1908; obviously, she survived the fire. (Members of the Oblak family emigrated to the United States in the early years of the twentieth century; hence they do not appear in the 1900 census.) John Sr. may have been searching for daughter Mary that night, but the child he lost was son John. The 1920 Federal Census lists a nine-year-old boy named John at the Oblak residence. The "John" listed was born in 1911, given the name of his dead older sibling.

Some of the accounts detailing incidents at the temporary morgue during the identification process come from Marshall Everett's book. The vast majority, however, have been culled from three of Cleveland's daily newspapers—the *Plain Dealer, Press,* and *News* (inclusive dates, March 5–7, 1908). I have taken the liberty of correcting misspellings of names that appeared in the original sources. Newspapermen, like census takers, wrote down what they thought they heard; hence Nils Thompson first appears in the press as "Mills" Thompson. Under these emotionally trying circumstances, a reporter generally would not ask, "Can you repeat that?" or "Could you spell that, please?" I have relied on the list of victims compiled by Mary Louise Jesek Daley of the Collinwood Nottingham Historical Society for the proper spelling of names.

The statistics detailing the work of the women from the Visiting Nurses' Association were supplied to the Collinwood Nottingham Historical Society by Emily Dubyoski, manager of communications and marketing. I am indebted to Elva Brodnick for passing the information on to me.

The *Plain Dealer* carried the poignant story of "Mrs. Maknic" on March 6. Whether the desperate woman lost a daughter named Mary is difficult to know. There is no Mary Maknic on the list of victims published by the Cleveland Public Library in 2008 or Mary Louise Jesek Daley's list; there are, however, a Josephine *Mahlic* on both the Cleveland Public Library's and Daley's lists, a *Mary* Marea on both the Cleveland Public Library's and Marshall Everett's lists, and a Jerca *Maria* Morelja only on Daley's list. Is either of these girls the missing daughter to whom the *Plain Dealer* article refers? Did the committee members and/or the paper simply get the names wrong? Unfortunately, it's virtually impossible to know; there are too many variants of Maknic or Mahlic in the relevant Cleveland City Directories and Federal Census.

The woman whom the *Press* identified by the name *Zeigler* was actually Mrs. Harry Sigler, mother of Mabel Sigler. (None of the victims' names that begin with *Z* are even remotely close to *Zeigler*.) As recounted in the text, husband Harry Sigler fought with Otto Markushatt over the identification of the girl's body, the latter insisting it was his daughter Elsie. This is, perhaps, one of the best examples of how misspellings and confusion over first names in the press has crippled attempts to arrive at a definitive list of victims. The Siglers buried the body as their daughter Mabel.

The parade of stories in the press about what may have been Katherine Weiler's body clearly demonstrates how difficult it can be for a historian to stitch together a simple, coherent narrative from newspaper stories. The Cleveland press ran four different reports involving what may have been or may not have not been Katherine Weiler's remains: first, the story of a body found in a tangled mass around 1:00 P.M.; second, the body that had been discovered and removed at the end of the day; third, Barney Reiche's claim that he personally placed her corpse on a stretcher; and, finally, the body that turned out to be the corpse of John Kranjnak. Were these four separate recoveries, or did they all refer to a single set of remains; and were any of those bodies the remains of Katherine Weiler? To add to the confusion, Gustav Weiler alleges in his memorial tribute that the body recovered and identified Thursday evening by Dr. Hill as his daughter had "disappeared" by Friday morning, suggesting a second body, ultimately identified as John Kranjnak.

The telegrams to members of the Weiler family, as well as Gustav Weiler's comments, are taken from his memorial tribute to his daughter.

The confusion over the gender of the body identified on Thursday evening as Katherine Weiler actually sparked the utterly absurd notion that Katherine Weiler was a cross-dressing man.

William Hubern Bullock was the motion picture photographer who also filmed slightly less than a minute of the smoldering school building in the aftermath of the fire.

Chapter Five

A TIME OF RECKONING

In 1908, Collinwood's population hovered around eight thousand. In such a small, relatively tight community, the deaths of 172 children in a single, terrible incident was devastating, almost beyond comprehension. Virtually an entire generation of Collinwood children had been wiped out. Many families suffered multiple losses; indeed, some lost all their children.

It's a part of human nature to believe that disasters don't just happen, they proceed from very simple, understandable causes. To believe otherwise is to accept the role of chaos in human affairs; someone or something must be at fault. In the hours and days following the tragedy, even as officialdom planned the formal investigations, city newspapers cataloged a number of off-the-cuff guesses as to the fire's origin, from a variety of sources. The finger of blame moved erratically from one potential target to the next. The three girls whom Fritz Hirter caught in the basement closet before the school day started were responsible. Teenage boys—street toughs hiding out in the basement to smoke—were the cause. Something in Hirter's closet was to blame. It was arson. Someone had deliberately and maliciously set the school ablaze. "School Was Set Afire Is Theory of Witness," roared the headline of a March 5 front-page *Press* article. "I am satisfied the fire was started by some person," insisted Dr. William H. Williams, Lake Shore surgeon and one of the first rescuers on the scene, "as there

A contemporary newspaper cartoon by Bob Satterfield. (Everett, *Complete Story of the Collinwood School Disaster*)

were no electric wires in the building and no gas pipes, and there were no pipes running through the closet, or near it."

An event as catastrophic as the Collinwood School Fire immediately puts enormous pressure on local and state officials on all levels who might have any oversight responsibilities. Deputy Fire Marshal Thrush in Columbus threatened criminal proceedings. Was there negligence? Was there any legal culpability? "Who will fix the responsibility, criminal or otherwise, if there is any?" demanded the *News*. "Who will take steps to punish whoever may have been guilty of negligence or carelessness in that connection?" On March 5, the *Plain Dealer* issued an ominous warning in its front-page headline, "Stern Hand to Fall on Those to Blame."

Was the architect somehow responsible? Was there something about either the layout of the building or the construction materials used? Had the school been properly inspected? If so, by whom? The state? Did the school board take the necessary steps to ensure that the building was being properly maintained? Who bore responsibility for daily operations and upkeep? Were they qualified? Were there periodic fire drills? If so, how many? How often? How quickly could the building be evacuated? And perhaps most important: just how vulnerable were other area schools? What steps were being taken to make sure something this terrible does not happen again?

The immediate aftermath of the Collinwood disaster spawned a flurry of official investigations both large and small. John H. Morgan, the chief inspector of workshops and factories in Columbus, thought the building's construction may have been faulty; hence on Thursday, March 5, Cleveland's fire department chief George Wallace and State Fire Marshal deputies Harry T. Brockman and Nathan Fiegenbaum were dispatched to Collinwood, where they met up with Building Inspector S. S. Lougee for a thorough inspection of the ruins. (The *Press* maintained that Brockman and Fiegenbaum actually interviewed Emma Neibert in the paper's editorial office the day of the fire.) Locally, two separate investigations—one by the school board, the other by the Cuyahoga County coroner—began probing the catastrophe immediately. The Collinwood city council announced with great fanfare that it would be investigating the disaster; school board president Philip Graf presided over what the *Plain Dealer* termed a "vigorous probe," while Coroner Thomas A. Burke of Cuyahoga County convened an official inquest at his Cleveland office, which began on Thursday, March 5, and ran through Tuesday, March 10. "Perhaps the law was violated at Collinwood, and that a charge of criminal carelessness may be made to stick against somebody," mused the *News*. "There is big work for the officials to do."

In retrospect, the school board inquiry, which began on March 4 at Clarke Avenue School at 7:00 P.M. and lasted until well beyond 1:00 A.M., seems a somewhat hastily arranged, perhaps ill-advised, affair. Understandably, the school board wanted to find the catastrophe's underlying cause as quickly as possible. If the fault lay in the design or construction of the building, other schools in the immediate metropolitan area might be equally at risk.

In 1908, however, no one understood how emotionally devastating the effects of a severe trauma could be on an individual. It would be another ten years before World War I gave the world the term *shell shock*, and it would be left to the waning years of the century to fully understand PTSD (post-traumatic stress disorder). In order to testify coherently before the school board within hours of the most horrific tragedy any of them had ever experienced, witnesses—among them the surviving teachers and janitor Fritz Hirter—had to come to terms emotionally with the unimaginable. On Friday, March 6, the *Plain Dealer* reported that the board's investigation would be suspended until all the funerals had taken place. By Sunday March 8, the board issued a statement that no one would be officially blamed and that the fire was, according to the *Plain Dealer*, "unavoidable." Board secretary J. R. Hauder further pointed out that testimony had made it clear that the boilers were in working order and that "conditions in the building were in first-class shape. Under the circumstances we cannot find that anybody was responsible for the fire."

The second major inquiry—formally designated as an investigation into the death of "Katherine Weiler, et al," case no. 11325—proved a much more carefully considered and executed affair. The evening of the fire, Coroner Burke began issuing subpoenas for witnesses to appear before him at his Lakeside Avenue office beginning at 10:00 A.M. the next day. Over the next few days, he summoned twenty-three individuals to testify at proceedings that lasted until Tuesday, March 10. Six of the seven surviving teachers received subpoenas the evening of March 4, ordering them to appear at the coroner's office on Friday, March 6. Some of the most significant witnesses, such as Emma Neibert and janitor Fritz Hirter (who lost three of his own children in the disaster), weren't called to appear until the following week, during the final two days of the proceedings, thus allowing at least some time for them to process the horror. The Cleveland press kept an ever-vigilant watch on all the official proceedings and reported on its findings at great length. Local papers, however, strove to find a simple answer for the disaster, and ultimately the city's four major dailies narrowed the quest for a villain down to three candidates: janitor Fritz Hirter, the Collinwood fire department, and the school building itself.

FRITZ HIRTER

The blame game began almost immediately; and, naturally enough, the first person to feel Collinwood's wrath was janitor Fritz Hirter, whose job it was to tend the furnaces and make sure that everything in the building was in proper working order. Hirter had suffered severe burns around his face and on his arms while trying to rescue the trapped pupils. Not only had he lost three of his own children, one of them died before his eyes, pleading for his help.

But extreme grief and uncontrollable rage require an outlet, so Hirter became the initial target of the neighborhood's desperately angry and sustained finger-pointing. Philip Gilbert, father of eleven-year-old

Janitor Fritz Hirter, photographed during the fire's aftermath. (Everett, *Complete Story of the Collinwood School Disaster*)

victim Alma, angrily told the *News*, "The janitor who had charge of the boiler had no skill in such matters. He has no business to manage a boiler. . . . [H]e don't know anything about boilers. I have known Hirter for 10 or 11 years. He was a florist in Germany." Gilbert's assertion about Hirter's former job is simply inaccurate. He was not a florist; he tended the boilers at a greenhouse. But the damage was done! A fact that had been inaccurately recalled and subsequently reported had become a damning element in a charge of incompetence.

Even if Hirter were ultimately cleared of any culpability in the disaster, the suggestion that he lacked the necessary qualifications for the job would linger. "I'll tell you how it started," Gilbert's wife chimed in. "That janitor made up a big fire and left the door open. The superintendent is to blame for hiring that janitor. He ought not to be there with all those children." Not only does her dismissive repetition of "that janitor" depersonalize Hirter, it suggests of underlying class or ethnic resentments in the neighborhood that were exacerbated by the tragedy. A second article in the *News* dealing with the Gilbert family loss and bearing the ominous title "Mother Weeps, Father Asks for Vengeance" quotes Harry Garities, brother-in-law of the victim, who insisted, "He has no license to manage a boiler. I have heard the rumors that he filled the furnace as full of coal as he possibly could, and then left it while he got a lunch. If he had any knowledge of running a furnace, he would have known better than that." Yet his wife, the victim's older sister (unidentified by name in the *News* article), cautioned, "Speak no ill of the poor janitor now. He himself has lost three little ones in the fire and the hand of God is already heavy upon him."

According to the *Press*, Coroner Burke was one of the first in local officialdom to cast a suspicious eye on Hirter. "Where Was Janitor? Is Burke's Inquiry," proclaimed the headline of a brief front-page article in the March 7 edition of the *Press*, supposedly written by the coroner himself. "The most important development in the investigation," the anonymous writer declared, "is the fact that one person has said Fritz Hirter, the school house janitor, was at his house when the fire started." The writer was referring to a piece of hearsay passed on to the *Press* by William Lee, chief of the Lake Shore fire department. Lee insisted that Julius Dietrich, a Lake Shore watchman, had informed him that his wife insisted Hirter often left the school for a couple hours at a time to do gardening. "She said," Lee told the *Press*, "she saw smoke coming from the basement windows when Hirter was running toward the school house." In a March 6 *News* article, however, Collinwood mayor Westropp immediately came to the janitor's defense. "Hirter is a careful and thoroughly responsible man. I don't believe he is guilty of any carelessness. He always took great pains with his work and did many unnecessary things to keep the school yard and building in good condition."

In a move of almost unimaginable insensitivity, the school board called Hirter to testify at its inquiry on the night of March 4. In the immediate aftermath of the fire, Deputy State Fire Marshal Brockman had questioned him about the layout of the school and the location of the exits—an on-site interview memorialized by at least two press photographs. Initially, Hirter thought arson must have been the cause. "The fire could not have possibly have started except through some person's deliberate and malicious act," he insisted to the *News*. Now, struggling with the pain of fresh burns, wrestling with his own grief and trauma, and perhaps well aware that the finger of blame was turning toward him, Hirter backed off his arson claim and tried to recount the events of that morning while enduring the stern, accusing stares of his neighbors and bereaved parents.

According to the *News*, most of his testimony dealt with the two school doorways—such matters as their dimensions, as well as how they were locked and under what circumstances. On the morning of March 6, the *Plain Dealer* recounted his agonized insistence that he did "not know how the fire started. If you were to kill me, I could not tell you. I do not know. I do not know." On the afternoon of March 5, the *News* quoted Hirter's assertion that no one had ever told him exactly how to put in a fire alarm. "I never gave a fire alarm before," he insisted. "I just went into Miss Irwin's room and pulled it three times. I never had any instructions about that, but had heard the principal give it a dozen times. My order is to open the doors as soon as I hear the alarm."

The *Press* and the *News* produced radically different—indeed, con-flicting—accounts of how Hirter handled himself as a witness the next day; it isn't clear whether this Thursday session was a continuation of the school board inquiry or a separate investigation launched by what the *News* termed "deputy state fire marshals and city officials." According to the *Press,* Hirter's answers to questions from the deputy marshal predictably became confused, and finally, around noon, the poor man broke down completely and "suddenly began shouting and screaming at the top of his voice." Ultimately, someone had to summon a physician to quiet the out-of-control Hirter.

On March 6, however, the *News* vigorously insisted that such a violent episode had never taken place and that, in spite of the *Press's* claim to the contrary, Hirter had remained relatively calm during the examination; but, again, the damage was done. Hirter's sanity had become a volatile issue for newspaper speculation and debate. The *News* stood firmly on Hirter's side. "Fritz Hirter is not insane," the paper proclaimed, insisting he had "borne up well under the strain of sorrow and investigations at which he has been a principal witness." The *Press,* however, continued to assert otherwise, claiming that on Thursday and Friday night, the man was such a nervous wreck that "opiates were used to quiet his cries of suffering." Assuming the claim is even accurate, the paper seems never to have considered that drugs might have been necessary to treat the pain of his burns, not his mental condition. "I am feeling pretty sick," Hirter confided to the *News.* "The burns about my head pain me terribly." The *Press's* rep-utation for sensationalism and going for the emotional jugular was apparently already well established. Once again, the *News* disputed the *Press* account, insisting its reporters had seen Hirter Thursday night, at which time "he was perfectly calm."

The journalistic war over Hirter's mental state apparently had little or no effect on the crowds of suspicious neighbors, bereaved families, and morbidly curious bystanders that continued to gather outside the Hirter home. Westropp ordered that a policeman stand guard at the Hirter residence and that other officers take up positions nearby in anticipation of any trouble. Perhaps predictably, the *Press* took a somewhat more sensational approach and noted that guards toting guns had been posted outside on the porch because "there have been indications of a smoldering flame of wrath against Hirter among the foreigners whose little ones lost their lives in the school . . . and ever since the fire there have been rumors—all of them, the officials now believe, without any foundation—that the janitor was not in the building." According to the afternoon daily, some of those on patrol outside the house were there to keep Hirter from hurting himself. The pressures on Fritz Hirter were virtually beyond comprehension. Investigators even pursued the poor, beleaguered janitor to his house Friday evening, pelting him with a barrage of questions while standing around his bed. The *Plain Dealer* subsequently reported that Westropp had grown so concerned about Hirter's safety that he thought it a good idea for him to leave Collinwood, at least for the time being. Hence, John Leffel, one of the mayor's neighbors, surreptitiously smuggled him out of his home and accompanied him to an undisclosed location on Cleveland's West Side, much to the annoyance of Marshal Brockman, who apparently spent considerable time trying to track Hirter down for further questioning.

Fritz Hirter buried three of his children in Lake View Cemetery on Friday, March 6, following a 10:00 A.M. service—presided over by Pastor William Friebolin—at the German Reformed church. There were only two caskets. Hirter's two young daughters, Helena and Ida, were buried together, while son Walter was placed in a separate casket. Reportedly, the crowds that still milled around the family home grew quiet as the two white caskets emerged. Although there had not been any specific threats, officials decided to err on the side of caution, so three deputy sheriffs accompanied Hirter from his home on Collamer, sat behind him and his wife as unobtrusively as possible during the church service, and even followed them to Lake View Cemetery. After all the formal proceedings, Hirter quietly slipped away to his temporary hiding place on the city's West Side. The *Press* noted that because of the triple funeral service, Coroner Burke had excused Hirter from testifying at the formal inquest—at least for the time being. Yet the paper continued to assert that Hirter's mental condition was at issue, insisting that he was far too upset to provide coherent testimony.

With the janitor out of the picture, or at least out of Collinwood and beyond the reach of reporters, the *Press* turned to his wife, a woman whom the paper termed "the saddest figure in Collinwood." On Monday, March 9, the afternoon daily devoted an entire article exclusively to Eliza Hirter, zeroing in on her grief and despair with overly wrought prose worthy of a pulp novelist. Although the piece's sentimentality is typical of the period, a modern-day reader would likely consider it a rather tasteless and unnecessary invasion of the poor woman's privacy. The paper described the distraught Mrs. Hirter as a "frail little woman" and a "little, bent woman." Furthermore, it insisted she was "sick in mind and body" and "tortured by the charges of neglect whispered all over Collinwood." A *Press* artist produced a heartrending drawing of the grieving woman sitting at a table strewn with the toys of her dead children, her open Bible before her, and a child clutched to her bosom. A verse from *Mathew* (19:14), reproduced in an appropriately gothic font, occupied the lower right hand corner of the drawing at the top of the page: "Suffer little children, and forbid them not to come unto Me; for of such is the kingdom of Heaven."

The *Press* painted a deeply disturbing picture of curious "visitors" streaming into the house and invading her privacy with thoughtless questions. "Do you think your husband was to blame for the fire? Did he set it himself?" On March 8, the school board absolved Hirter of any responsibility. In a page two article, "Board to Blame No One for Fire," board secretary J. R. Hauder maintained, "The testimony shows clearly that the janitor was in the building attending to his duties when the fire broke out."

The evening of March 4, Coroner Burke had begun to issue subpoenas for a formal inquest, to begin the next morning at his office at the morgue in downtown Cleveland. "It would not do for me to say anything about the Collinwood horror at this time," Burke told the *Plain Dealer*. "I have spent many hours today at the scene of the tragedy and the machinery of my office was at once set in motion for an exhaustive investigation." Though one can sense the seasoned politician in his utterance, his carefully worded statement is exactly what one would expect from a public official preparing to investigate such a monumental tragedy. But it raises questions about the validity of the March 7 *Press* article—supposedly written by the man himself—in which Burke allegedly questioned exactly where Hirter was when the fire started. The brief article seems rather inflammatory and is clearly at odds with the cautious statement to the *Plain Dealer* the night of March 4. Did Burke really write the *Press* article, or is this another example of the paper's yellow journalism?

Julius Dietrich's wife, Olga—the original source of the claim that Hirter was not at the school when the fire started—finally testified at the coroner's inquest on Monday, March 9, and her statements did not exactly correlate with those her husband had allegedly already made. "I saw Hirter on his side porch," she insisted. "I can't tell what time it was. It was about ten minutes before the fire started. When I saw Hirter I supposed he had come home to lunch. . . . When I next saw Hirter he was running out the back door of the school house. The building was then on fire. He carried a long poker and ran to the front doors and broke out the glass in them."

Burke issued a subpoena for Fritz Hirter to appear downtown at the inquest on Monday morning, March 9, at 10:00 A.M., thus allowing the beleaguered janitor at least a couple of days to collect himself. He began by reciting a list of his daily duties and responsibilities. He testified that it was his habit to go home for lunch between 10:00 and 10:40 A.M. (the fire had started at 9:30) and return around 11:10. After recounting his actions from the moment Emma Neibert alerted him to the smoke, he vehemently denied he had ever left the building before the fire—except for three or four minutes he spent in the orchard at the back of the school.

According to the *Plain Dealer* on March 10, at the end of his testimony the coroner addressed Hirter, clearing him of any responsibility. "I want to take this occasion to say publicly that the people of Collinwood have no reason to blame you. You did not only your duty but you did more than your duty. Your conduct is to be commended. In addition you have told the truth, I believe, every time you have told your story." The final verdict of the inquest restated the coroner's belief in Hirter's innocence. "We further find that Mr. Fred [*sic*] Hirter, the janitor in charge of said School building was present in the building at the time the said fire was discovered and that said Fred Hirter faithfully and expeditiously carried out his duties in the emergency." But the cloud of possible guilt would hang over Hirter's head and follow him in the decades after the disaster. Seventy years after the fire, survivor Joseph Konst continued to fix blame on Hirter. "He would walk home and have a cup of tea or coffee," he told *Plain Dealer* reporter Wally Guenther in 1978. "Then he would return to ring the recess bell about 10:00 A.M. If the janitor had been in the building around 9:00 A.M., he might have prevented the tragedy."

THE COLLINWOOD FIRE DEPARTMENT

The undermanned, ill-equipped, inadequately trained twenty-man volunteer Collinwood fire department immediately became an easy and convenient target. "Fire Is Victorious Over Leaky Hose," screamed a *Plain Dealer* story headline on Friday, March 6. "Spasmodic Engine Puffs and Wheezes during Struggle of Death." The morning daily mocked the "wheezy gasoline engine" and the horse-drawn hose wagon that "squeaked and rattled as it struck the numerous ruts in the mire of the road." "And this was the fire department," the paper scoffed, "depended upon to protect a town of 7,000 inhabitants, forty-three miles of streets and property worth several millions."

The ongoing question of Collinwood's annexation to Cleveland proper—a proposed action that local officials and Collinwood residents had debated and approved—became a major factor in the examination of the fire department's inadequacies. Political wrangling and maneuvering had delayed the expected merger, and with the promise of Cleveland's far greater financial resources looming in the future, those who controlled the village's purse strings had grown reluctant to spend any money on civic improvements. The catastrophe at Lakeview Elementary School renewed the debate and propelled it into high gear. "Annexation talk was rife yesterday at city hall," proclaimed the *Plain Dealer* on March 8. "The opinion was expressed by city councilmen and

Collinwood's wholly inadequate gas fire engine. (Everett, *Complete Story of the Collinwood School Disaster*)

others that the sooner the annexation of all the adjoining suburbs is consummated the better it will be for the general community." Sadly, it often takes a major tragedy to spur politicians into official action; Collinwood became part of Cleveland in 1910.

Though city papers touted the advantages of the far more sophisticated and professional Cleveland fire department, it remains questionable how effective the admittedly better-equipped city firefighters could have been. The fire started around 9:30 and grew with such rapidity that by the time Cleveland fire department's Battalion Chief Michael F. Fallon arrived at the school, at 10:50, "the building was doomed." Cleveland fire department's Chief George A. Wallace sadly concurred. Though he had sent a steam fire engine, which had arrived shortly after the local Collinwood brigade finally managed to get to the scene, "it was too late to be of any service," Wallace lamented to the *Press*. "The building was then a mass of flames and part of the floors had fallen." On Friday, March 6, Collinwood school superintendent Frank P. Whitney testified before the coroner's inquest. "I doubt if any fire department in the world could have done any kind of effective work."

THE BUILDING

Lakeview Elementary School, itself, also became a target for the daily press. The impressive building that stood on Collamer was quite new. Built originally in 1901 in response to the rapidly growing local population of school-age children, the building was considered state-of-the-art. It was the sort of schoolhouse one could find almost anywhere in early twentieth-century America, especially in rural areas. By 1907, however, overcrowding had necessitated a major expansion; but even the addition of four new rooms proved a stopgap measure insufficient to deal with the exploding neighborhood population of elementary-age students. By 1908, there were nine classes whose sizes ranged from the upper thirties to the mid-forties—figures that would horrify a modern-day educator—and the third-floor "attic" had been pressed into serving the entire fifth grade.

The *News* led the charge against the building. "The fire proved the schoolhouse to have been a deathtrap in its construction," the paper insisted in a late edition on March 4, "and full investigation may prove that somebody's blunder . . . contributed to the terrible fatality among the 360 children who, penned in by the flames, found the only possible exit cut off to them in their panic and fear." Coroner Burke contributed to the assault, proclaiming the construction of the school an "outrage."

Yet the building had been deemed a good insurance risk after its January 1907 inspection. Working through the Cleveland Insurance Agency, Collinwood had insured the school for a total of $28,000, approximately 80 percent of its estimated value from three separate agencies: the Insurance Company of North America, the Fidelity Fire Insurance Company, and the German Alliance. State Building Inspector John H. Morgan insisted to the *News* that, given the then current state of the law, the school would most likely have passed inspection. "If I had inspected the school building in Collinwood the day before the fire, I should probably have approved it. Under the present laws of the state I could do nothing else." The problems, he maintained, rested with the manner in which fire drills were conducted and the then current state of building code regulations. "It is certain that if the fire drills had been extended to the use of the fire escape there would not have been anywhere near the terrible loss of life." He further proposed that buildings should be outfitted with shafts through which children could slide to safety—an escape mechanism that had been employed in Canadian schools since the 1800s. When Morgan turned his attention to the building, he declared, "I favor a law which

The Collinwood School Fire prompted school safety concerns all over the country. This cartoon was originally printed in the April 1908 issue of the *American School Board Journal.*

would require all new school buildings to be made fireproof and in my opinion the basements of all present buildings where the heating apparatus is should be protected by fireproofing."

The initial examination of the unstable ruins by Cleveland fire department's Chief Wallace and Deputy State Fire Marshals Brockman and Fiegenbaum placed most of the blame on the building materials employed for the school's interior, the placement of the steam pipes, and the configuration of the interior space—preliminary results that the ongoing series of investigations would expand upon and largely confirm. Inspectors found the Georgia pine used for the stairways and other interior features to have been "dry as tinder," even though the building was relatively new. That the janitor routinely used oil to clean the stairs only added to the building's combustibility.

According to the March 6 *Plain Dealer*, virtually none of the wood survived the fire. The paper also noted that the steam pipes that delivered the building's heat had been placed only two inches from large, heavy wooden joists. "The heat had dried the timbers until a spark would have set them aflame. Sections of the steam pipes leading to the upper rooms had almost kiln dried stairways and woodwork. Joists near the boilers, subjected to the heat of almost all the steam pipes in the building, had even burned far into the brick walls." On March 8, Wallace told the *Plain Dealer*, "The heat from the pipes coming through the plaster coverings baked the woodwork overhead. The building may have been slowly burning for weeks." Wallace's theory received unexpected support from W. S. Wilson, superintendent of school buildings and grounds in Marion, Ohio. That city's State Street School had originally been outfitted with a heating system similar to Lakeview Elementary's. According to a March 8 *Plain Dealer* article, the old system had been replaced with a newer model in early 1908. When workers tore out the wooden flooring, they discovered that parts of it and the wooden joists had been charred in a number of places, leading Marion officials to believe that there actually had been a fire at the school but that it had been smothered due to a lack of a draft before anyone noticed it.

THE MYTH OF THE INWARD-SWINGING DOORS

Mention the Collinwood School Fire today to anyone even vaguely aware of the disaster, and his or her eyes will glimmer with recognition. You then will be told that the high number of deaths was attributable to the building's doors opening inward and, moreover, the fact that today all school doors swing outward can be traced back directly to the mandated improvements put in place as a result of that catastrophe. It's an attractive and admittedly logical notion, and the widely held belief can be traced back to the initial newspaper coverage of the incident. But it is a myth.

In spite of over one hundred years of repeated attempts to set the record straight, the notion that the doors swung inward remains an integral part of the Collinwood School Fire story; and this unfortunate piece of misinformation began the day of the fire. Newspaper articles and off-the-cuff remarks battled with sworn testimony. In its evening edition, the *Press* declared, "The panic-stricken children rushed to the rear door, which opened inward. They massed against it until it was jammed tightly shut." The next day, a *Plain Dealer* article, bearing the headline "Doors Are Blamed for Loss of Life," repeated the claim, quoting Deputy State Fire Marshal Fiegenbaum. "The doors of the North Collinwood school opened toward the inside." Fiegenbaum had arrived at the site while the fire was still burning, and he was the only representative from the state fire marshal's office to explore the ruins on March 4.

The details of that brief article make it abundantly clear that Fiegenbaum made a snap judgment based on a cursory examination of the still-smoldering building. "By means of inquires among bystanders and by inspection of such parts of the ruins *as had cooled sufficiently to permit entrance* he conducted an investigation. The excitement made his work difficult, and he was unable to secure a great deal of definite information with regard to the origin of the fire" (emphasis mine). Millard J. Wilson, a member of the Collinwood fire department, also maintained that the doors swung inward.

School principal Anna Moran, however, refuted the claim almost immediately. She was quoted in the March 5 edition of the *Plain Dealer*: "It is not true that the doors opened toward the inside." On March 6, the *News* backed Moran's claim, reporting that an examination of the building's original plans "shows that all doors opened outward." But the damage was done; the myth of the inward-swinging doors had firmly taken hold. Marshall Everett probably gave the piece of misinformation its greatest boost when he wrote in his 1908 book, "This door, like the one in front, opened inward." The story of the inward-swinging doors has been repeated ever since the day of the fire and stubbornly persists into the twenty-first century.

In 1938, the erroneous piece of folklore received a major challenge. Director of Cleveland Schools James F. Brown learned that the koi pond that had been an integral part of the memorial garden installed on the site of the disaster between 1916 and 1918—twenty years old in 1938—was beginning to disintegrate. He promptly ordered workers to tear out what remained of the old structure and replace it with a new pool. As the men excavated, they uncovered remnants of the building's foundation. "To give us a record," Brown explained to the *Plain Dealer*, "I ordered the whole foundation exposed. I thought if we could reconstruct the building, we might discover some flaws which existed which should not exist in modern buildings. In short, I thought we could learn something from this horrible experience."

Unfortunately, Brown's proposed reconstruction proved an extremely difficult task. Since the school had been built before Collinwood's annexation to Cleveland, the board of education did not have a copy of the original blueprints. Led by Brown and the board's chief architectural draftsman, Arthur Baer, a select group of men delved into what they saw as the enduring mystery of the Collinwood School Fire. They consulted books, read old newspaper articles, examined the now-exposed foundation, and consulted the inquest testimony, all in an attempt to understand how the catastrophe unfolded. They also interviewed Fritz Hirter, eight years into his retirement and still living on East 152nd Street at his old address. Essentially, they arrived at the same conclusions that local officials had thirty years before. The building's doors did swing outward. The appallingly high loss of life could be attributed to other factors: the narrow wooden stairways, the narrow vestibule at the foot of the stairs, and the partitions to which the doors had been attached. But the myth of the inward-swinging doors was too deeply entrenched, and it has easily survived coordinated assault on its veracity.

Since the fire began in janitor Fritz Hirter's basement closet beneath the doors opening to the east, that means of egress became blocked by the flames almost immediately. Thus, virtually all of the subsequent attention has always been focused on the doors that faced west. The intense, long-running argument over the direction in which the doors swung has tended to obscure two other equally significant questions: First, were the doors sufficiently wide to allow easy passage? And second, were they locked? Chief Wallace weighed in on the first question almost immediately, as reported in the *Press* on March 6. In a relatively brief article that the paper attributed to Wallace, the chief asserted, "The loss of life in the Collinwood school would not have been so great had there been no partitions at the sides of the storm doors at the rear entrance of the building."

He pointed out that the hallway that led from the bottom of the staircase to the vestibule was ten feet, eight inches wide. Common sense would dictate, he argued, that the exit from the building should be equally as wide. But it was not! "Two feet eight inches on either side had been taken off for the partitions on which the doors were hung"— thus effectively reducing the width of the exit to slightly more than five feet. Wallace repeated his assertions to the *News* the same day. "The school authorities should have made the back outer and inner doors the full width of something over 10 feet. Instead they narrowed the doors to about six feet and filled the remaining space in with wooden partitions. This left a very narrow margin at the foot of the stairs for the children to escape."

The question as to whether the doors were locked applies mainly to the inner doors of the west exit. Supposedly, the inner set always remained unlocked, even when the school was closed. Obviously, the doorway on the right, in which the pupils became wedged, was clear;

it was open on the day of the fire. All the disagreement pertains to the status of the door on the left: Was it open? If so, who opened it and when? Was it locked? If so, how and when did it become locked? It was clearly locked at the height of the fire; rescuers testified that it could not be opened, in spite of men pounding on it with their fists and throwing themselves against it.

Marshal Fiegenbaum, as mentioned, was the first state official on the scene and insisted to the *News* on March 5 that the door in question was locked, and his words bore the weight of his authority. Unfortunately, the subsequent testimony at both the school board inquiry and the coroner's inquest, as recorded in Cleveland's four major dailies, emerges as a Gordian knot of contradictions that neither paper attempted to clarify. The phrases *left-hand door* and *right-hand door* are used casually. But how are these designations meant to be understood within the context of the testimony: right or left if one is facing outward from the school's interior, or standing outside looking in?

It is often not clear whether the witness is referring to the inner or outer set of doors, and the terminology employed simply adds to the confusion: words such as *latched, bolted,* and *locked* are tossed about freely, as if they were synonyms. And while all these designations may accurately describe a door that could not be opened, they clearly suggest different modes of rendering it impassable. Similarly, the terms *hooked back* and *fastened* get a fairly healthy workout, totally free of any specificity. Witnesses often appear to be using the word *open* as if it meant *unlocked.* At the school board inquiry on the evening of March 4, Emma Neibert maintained that both the inner and outer left-hand doors were "always kept latched." She also insisted, "Mr. Hirter was kicking and pulling trying to get the inside door open. Miss Rose was trying, too; but they couldn't open it." Katherine Gollmar had run around to the west side of the building after descending the fire escape, but she was also unable to budge the closed door.

Fritz Hirter testified at the coroner's inquest on March 9 that all the doors were kept open (unlocked?) during school hours. On March 5, the *News* recounted Hirter's testimony at the school board inquiry the previous evening: "I went and opened the doors. All the outside doors were closed. One was bolted at each entrance. There was never any way of fastening the left hand doors back." On March 9, however, the paper reported on Hirter's testimony at the coroner's inquest in which he alleged that he "hooked back" the left-hand door and that it somehow became closed after Miss Lynn's class had escaped.

Though city newspapers dutifully passed on what witnesses said at the various hearings, it remains virtually impossible to construct a coherent, precise narrative concerning the doors from the testimonial jumble that followed the tragedy. The witnesses called to testify at the school board inquiry that convened that same evening and ran into the early hours of the next morning had just emerged from one of the most horrifying experiences imaginable. The surviving teachers had lost two colleagues, struggled to save as many of their charges as possible, and watched helplessly as sheer panic drove a staggeringly high number of students to an awful death. Emma Neibert lost two siblings in the blaze and had witnessed the furious struggle to rescue the children jamming the west-facing doors. Fritz Hirter lost three of his children and sustained severe burns to his face and hands. It was ludicrous to expect detailed and accurate memories from individuals so severely traumatized. "The sight I witnessed in the hallway was terrible," reported Anna Moran at the school board inquiry. "I cannot begin to describe it."

It remains beyond dispute that all the doors of Lakeview Elementary School opened outward; it also remains clear that the interior left-hand door was either closed from the beginning of the evacuation or became closed at some unspecified point. Assuming that the door in question had been opened initially and was closed later, as Fritz Hirter maintained, why was it impossible to reopen it once it had closed?

The explanation I offer here is admittedly supposition, but it does address the issues of how the door was "bolted" or "latched" and why it could not be opened from the outside once it had closed. The door locked with a spring bolt—placed at the top of the door on its inward side—that slid into a hole at the top of the frame. Once secured, it could be opened only by pulling the spring bolt down and pushing the door outward. The door and the catch at the top of the frame would be beveled so the bolt would slide easily into place and lock simply by pulling the door closed. Assuming the door had been open, it could easily have slammed shut when someone fell against it from the outside. The wind was coming from the northeast that day, and the fire created a draft in the building's interior that blew toward the west exit. It is, therefore, highly unlikely that the door could have blown shut. Once closed, the door could be opened only by pulling the spring bolt down from the inside and pushing the door outward.

. . .

The coroner's findings regarding the causes of the fire and the reasons for the staggering death toll were clearly articulated and listed in the final verdict. For the most part, the official document put an end to speculations concerning the possibility of arson and attempts to charge Fritz Hirter with negligence. The verdict does not even mention the doors to the building, so the document is not the source of the notion that the doors opened inward. The entire conclusion appears below. Unfortunately, the legalese in which the document is rendered—especially concerning the word *failure*—gives the impression that the children were somehow to blame for what happened.

> Upon exhaustive inquiry, we are of the opinion that the fire which destroyed said Lakeview School, originated in a closet in the basement of said building, located under the front stairs or exit: that the said fire was caused by the overheating of the wooden joist of the first floor of said building, located over above described closet: that after the fire had been discovered and alarm had been given and the pupils had begun to hastily file out, the pupils using the rear exit, became in some unknown manner, "jammed" and congested in the rear stairway and thereby obstructed their own and exit of others that owing to this jam and congestion, the exit of the children could not be facilitated and with the spreading of the fire, the clothes and bodies of those jammed on the rear steps, became ignited and causing the burns which resulted in their deaths.
>
> We further find that Mr. Fred Hirter, the janitor in charge of said School building was present in the building at the time the said fire was

discovered and that said Fred Hirter, on discovery of the fire, duly gave the fire alarm and opened both the front and rear doors and otherwise, faithfully and expeditiously carried out his duties in the emergency.

In our opinion, the awful mortality connected with the burning of Lakeview School, Collinwood, can be attributed, first[:] To the excitement of the children due to the fire and the failure of the children to complete their exit in order: Second[:] In some degree, to the presence of the partition, located on the inside of the rear door of the school building, which cut off two or more feet on either side of the exit and impeded the exit of the children: Third[:] Because of the failure of the children to complete their exit in order and the faulty construction of the inner partition at the rear door, the children became jammed and congested on the rear steps and were thus unable to escape from the building.

NOTES

Joseph Konst's memory was inaccurate. According to his own testimony at the coroner's inquest, Hirter was in the building at 9:00 and at 9:30 A.M. when the fire started. Contrary to Konst's assertion, the janitor did not leave for lunch until at least 10:00. Confusion about the exact time various witnesses reported seeing Hirter around his house on March 4 has dogged the Collinwood School Fire story from the very beginning,

Coroner Burke issued four subpoenas: two on March 4, one on March 7, and a final one on March 8. The first subpoena called for six individuals to testify at the coroner's office on Thursday, March 5:

1. William H. Williams (a Lake Shore physician and one of the first on the scene)
2. Robert Gardner
3. William (illegible)
4. Philip Graf (president of the school board)
5. Harry H. Gage (clerk)
6. Joseph Anders (carpenter)

The second subpoena called for eight individuals, including six of the seven surviving teachers, to appear on Friday, March 6:

1. Ethel Rose (kindergarten: southeast corner, first floor)
2. Katherine Gollmar (fourth grade: northwest corner, second floor)

3. Lulu Rowley (third grade: southeast corner, second floor)
4. Laura Bodey (fifth grade: third floor)
5. Anna Moran (sixth grade and school principal: northeast corner, second floor)
6. Ruby Irwin (first grade: northeast corner, first floor)
7. Julius Dietrich (Lake Shore watchman who testified about Fritz Hirter's whereabouts at the time of the fire)
8. Frank P. Whitney (Collinwood school superintendent).

The third subpoena called for six to testify on March 9:

1. Olga Dietrich (wife of Julius Dietrich, who claimed she saw Fritz Hirter at his home at the time of the fire)
2. George A. Wallace (chief of Cleveland fire department)
3. George (Gregor?) Hammel (chief of Collinwood fire department)
4. Fritz Hirter (school janitor)
5. John Leffel (one of the first rescuers on the scene)
6. Wallace Upton (one of the first rescuers on the scene).

The fourth subpoena called for only three witnesses on March 10:

1. Emma Neibert (fourteen-year-old pupil, the first to notice signs of the fire)
2. Julius Neibert (Emma Neibert's father, who lost two children in the fire)
3. Frank J. Dorn (member of the school board, one of the first rescuers on the scene).

Chapter Six

AFTERMATH

If industry regulations are written in blood, building codes and design improvements rise from the ashes of disaster. A catastrophe as devastating as the Collinwood School Fire naturally raised concerns about the safety of other area school buildings, and the *Press* immediately launched its own investigation into the design and the physical condition of the city's educational facilities. How safe were local children when they walked through the schoolhouse doors? What dangers lurked in the dark corners of area school buildings far older than Lakeview Elementary? On Friday, March 6, the paper drew attention to a fire drill at Lawn Avenue School that had gone somewhat awry the day before. One of the double swinging doors leading out of the building initially refused to open as the lines of students marched toward it. When the paper indignantly pointed out that the school had no fire escapes, Principal May French obstinately argued that they were really not necessary: "The obedience of the children in case of fire is far more important than fire escapes."

The *Press* had investigated the safety of city schools two years before, in 1906, and found many of them wanting in a variety of ways. "Sixteen Thousand Children in Peril," roared its headline on May 16; "Death Sure in Case of School Fires." In October of the same year, the paper followed up its investigation by pointing out that some buildings had not held a fire drill since the school year had begun. Two years later, as the full horror of the Collinwood disaster unfolded, the paper revisited that investigation and renewed its assault on Cleveland's schools. "'Get Busy Quick!' Is 'Press' Advice to School Officials," the paper declared on March 9. "It took 170 dead Collinwood school children to impress Cleveland school officials that the safety of the children under their charge is more important than organizing the school janitors and other male employees for political action."

It would be decades before *Press* editor Louis B. Seltzer molded the paper into a sometimes overly aggressive social crusader, but even in 1908 the paper's yellow journalistic flare was evident. On March 9, it bellowed, "'The Press' demands, on behalf of every parent and child in this city, that the school authorities follow up their loud talk about what they are going to do by starting at once and not stopping until it is done." In a flurry of righteous anger, the paper launched a cavalcade of demands and threats: "Let it be possible to say truthfully 'THERE IS NOT A SCHOOL HOUSE IN CLEVELAND LESS SAFE THAN MONEY CAN MAKE IT.' The 'Press' gives notice NOW to every school official in this city that so far as its influence may go, it will make it so almighty hot for any of them who do not do their full duty in this matter that they will be sorry they ever went into public life."

Police prosecutor Ben Feniger threatened to issue arrest warrants for the entire board of education if it did not move immediately to close down Mayflower and Outhwaite Schools. "Both are of faulty and antiquated wooden construction," he told the *News*. "The stairways are arranged poorly and are all of wood. It would be an easy matter for a fire to start in any of a number of places in the furnace rooms in the basement."

On Friday, March 6, spurred by their own sense of civic responsibility, the *Press*'s fury, and, no doubt, Feniger's threats, Director of Cleveland Schools Charles Orr, Superintendent of Buildings J. C. Quayle, and three other building officials began a careful inspection of Cleveland's schools. Building Inspector S. S. Lougee didn't find any of the buildings to be in as dire shape as Feniger had alleged. He reported that while none of them were actually dangerous, no building was entirely safe; all needed extensive modernization. The amount of work and rehabilitation was enormous. Some of the Cleveland schools had been built in the mid-nineteenth century; many had no fire escapes. Some suffered from the same interior design and construction flaws that had plagued Lakeview Elementary School. Ever since he took office, Orr insisted, he had been lobbying for the removal of wooden partitions from Cleveland school buildings but was told by building architects that the structures were necessary to facilitate heating, that the open hallways could not be kept warm without them. In response to these preliminary findings, the board of education voted on issuing bonds worth of a total of $460,000, a sum large enough to cover the cost of improvements mandated by fire marshals and building inspectors.

The *Press* deployed an army of reporters—the size of which remained unspecified—to "inspect" city schools on Friday, March 6, and Saturday, March 7. Having no particular training in safety procedures or building design, the detachment tended to confine itself to such obviously observable details as the presence of fire escapes and the number of exits. On Monday, March 9, the paper announced the results of its two-day survey. "'Press' Investigation Discovers School Vestibules Closed by Partitions; Alterations Are Ordered by Director." Of the twenty schools canvased, four had been built in the mid-nineteenth century. Five lacked fire escapes, and four included the same sort of wooden partitions that contributed to the death toll in Collinwood. Most of the others suffered, in varying degrees, from a catalogue of structural woes. Alabama School at East Seventy-Sixth Street and St. Clair had "a death trap at the front entrance." One of the doors of Detroit School, near West Eighteenth Street, proved exceptionally difficult to open. Orchard School at Orchard Street and Forty-Second Street had six wooden stairways rather like those at Lakeview Elementary School. Some of the schools lacking fire escapes were multistory structures with huge enrollments. Four-story Central High served seventeen hundred pupils.

School officials deployed gangs of workers throughout the Cleveland system on Saturday, March 7, to begin a massive remodeling project. "We will not stop," Orr declared to the *Press* on March 7, "until every school building in Cleveland is as safe as it is possible for money to make it." Some of the mandated modifications were relatively simple and an obvious response to the Collinwood disaster; every wooden partition in school vestibules that even remotely resembled those in Lakeview Elementary School would be torn out by Monday, March 9.

Other proposed changes may have seemed like good ideas but would be exceedingly expensive, time-consuming, and difficult to accomplish. Each first-floor classroom would be outfitted with a glass door, while each second-floor room would have a glass door that opened directly on to the fire escape. In retrospect, a few of the proposed changes seem more like silly knee-jerk responses to the tragedy than carefully reasoned safety precautions. Guards were to be placed at the doors of schools deemed unsafe until remodeling had been completed, and pupils would march out of school each day to the beat of a drum.

Inevitably, the frenzy of concern over the safety of city schools spread to Cleveland's private schools as well. Fire wardens descended on private institutions, unearthing a trove of problems—including doors that were locked and did, indeed, swing inward. This multibuilding examination resulted in a series of retroactive amendments to the building codes that were to be drawn up before the evening of Monday, March 9. After examining the Temple at East Fifty-Fifth Street and Central Avenue, Feniger threatened to cancel the institution's Sunday school classes unless improvements were made. "Eight hundred and fifty children were in attendance in the school classes on the second and third floors of the building Sunday afternoon," he raged to the *News* on March 9. "There are eight rooms on the second floor and seven rooms on the third floor. There are two stairways leading from the Sunday school but only one exit. There are no fire escapes." Feniger summoned the building's owners to his office Monday morning and extracted promises "to do their utmost to have their contracts for fire escapes completed by Thursday [March 12] and to begin work immediately."

Clearly on a mission, the outraged prosecutor also turned his attention to eighteen downtown buildings lacking fire escapes and ordered their owners to appear at his office at 8:15 Monday morning. His dragnet succeeded in snaring some of the most august names of Cleveland society, such as Mrs. Samuel Mather, joint owner of the Western Reserve building at Superior Avenue and West Ninth Street. In a not-so-subtle display of power and anger, Feniger threatened to issue warrants against those who did not initiate plans for the installation of fire escapes within twenty-four hours of the Monday morning meeting.

As the investigations pushed forward under the sometimes distorting lens of city newspapers, Chief George Wallace of the Cleveland fire department emerged as one of the more reliable and sensible sources of information. He had responded immediately to the alarm on March 4; he had been with the fire marshals and the other state and local inspectors as they surveyed the damage of the still-smoldering ruin and pronounced the school "a veritable fire trap." That same day, he testified at the school board inquiry, where he became the first expert to assert that the cause of the fire was most likely overheated steam pipes placed too close to the building's wooden supports.

According to the March 6 *Plain Dealer,* Cleveland school authorities asked Wallace to "take charge of all school fire drills and bring them to the highest possible plane of efficiency." He and/or his deputies would be given the power to enter any school at any time and order a fire drill. Student monitors were to be assigned to guard every door and window that could serve as a point of egress—although it was not made clear whether this was to be a full-time assignment, to be carried out throughout the entire day, or a post to be filled only during drills.

Predictably, the aftermath of the Collinwood tragedy spawned a torrent of official and unofficial investigations, demands for improved building standards, public pronouncements from a variety of bully pulpits, and threats of all sorts of legal action. It all made for wonderful newspaper copy, and Cleveland's major dailies responded with well-honed journalistic instincts. One could be forgiven for assuming that every advancement in school design and execution can be traced to the aftermath of the Collinwood School Fire. However, it remains difficult to gage how many of these proposed and/or mandated safety measures were actually implemented. Considering the depth of the catastrophe, city papers reported each new development and declaration with the fanfare it deserved, but follow-up on a story was rare unless developments occurred immediately. The press tended to remain silent as to whether any of these improvements were initiated, especially over the long term. When the story broke, it was news; the next day, it was ancient history.

News of the Collinwood disaster spread across the entire country, providing determined reformers and, no doubt, a few opportunistic politicians with a convenient pulpit from which to preach the necessity for immediate reform in school construction. In a speech at the thirteenth annual meeting of the National Fire Protection Association in 1909, the organization's president, C. M. Goddard, worried that the country would soon lose interest and that the current vocal demands for needed reform would simply fade away. In author Casey C. Grant's words, Goddard called Americans "the most careless, indifferent, and unashamed people on Earth, ready to forget the spasms of horror soon after they occurred." Whether he was aware of it or not, Goddard echoed concerns raised in a March 6, 1908, *Plain Dealer* article that linked the Collinwood catastrophe with two other infamous and deadly fires in the early years of the twentieth century. "A year from now, if reminded of the Collinwood disaster, you will perhaps say, 'Oh yes, a schoolhouse burned down—did it not—and some children died in the flames,' in the same questioning tones that you would today recall the Slocum disaster, the Iroquois disaster, or any other great disaster that has shocked the world in recent years. You are shocked; you feel a real, if impersonal, grief—but it is easy to forget." But such a casual memory lapse did not occur; the reforms sparked by the Collinwood disaster proved immediate and long-lasting. Wood was banished from the list of interior building materials; walls were now brick or stone, stairways concrete and iron. Fire drills became mandatory; interior designs provided for more effect escape routes; and doorways were significantly widened. Spurred into action by the 1903 Iroquois Theater Fire in Chicago, Carl Prinzler teamed with architectural engineer Henry DuPont to develop a door that could be easily and quickly opened from the inside even when locked from the outside. The first model, produced by the Vonnegut Hardware Company, appeared in 1908. The "crash bar" or "panic bar" soon became a standard feature on exit doors on all public buildings, not just schools.

. . .

A week following the Collinwood disaster, ads in Cleveland papers invited interested and curious city residents to the America Theater—presumably a part of the American Amusement Company at 716 Superior Avenue—to see film of the catastrophe. Twenty-three-year-old William Hubern Bullock, a "moving picture operator" at the company, had shot the footage. When the initial reports of the fire spread to Cleveland proper on the morning of March 4, Bullock had grabbed his equipment and hopped a streetcar out to Collinwood. Newspaper reporters had noted his presence on the scene but had either lumped him in with the bevy of still photographers attracted to the disaster or had mentioned him only in passing. At a time when the succession of funerals was barely over or, perhaps, still going on, Bullock (or his employer) was offering Clevelanders the chance to see a film record of the catastrophe. In light of outraged protests from both Collinwood and city residents who found the whole enterprise appalling, Cleveland's Police Chief Fred Kohler summarily shut the operation down.

In 2008, the hundredth anniversary of the tragedy, the Cleveland Public Library discovered approximately two minutes of Bullock's silent film in the archives of the Motion Picture, Broadcasting, and Recorded Sound division at the Library of Congress. Shown for the first time in a century as part of library's anniversary remembrance, the film is now readily available on YouTube. Obviously, no one would pay to see barely two minutes of film in a downtown theater; these fragments clearly represent only a fraction of what Bullock most likely shot. The fate of the rest of the footage is unknown.

. . .

A photograph taken on Tuesday, March 10, documents that the scorched outer walls of the school were still standing—a grim, ruined, blackened memorial surrounding what had once been the building's basement, now filled with the debris from the collapsed interior and the unrecovered ashes of trapped students. When the land was finally reclaimed, the Collinwood school board faced the problem of what to do with it. Sources differ as to the options the board actually considered. Though some suggest that the plan was to simply rebuild the school on the same spot, others maintain that officials pursued the idea of selling the land.

Whatever the case may have been, the board's proposed plan immediately set off a storm of intense opposition. On March 4, 1968, the *News* revisited those sixty-year-old protests. Mothers who had lost children in the catastrophe came before the board dressed in black to vigorously protest. "The land is sacred to me," declared one grieving mother. Another defiantly proclaimed, "It can never be obliterated." "Surely, we don't want to run the risk of having a saloon built on the site," bluntly argued a third. (This last statement would seem to make it clear that the board's obvious intention was to sell the land.)

Faced with such vigorous opposition, the board relented. A new elementary school, appropriately named Memorial School, was built during 1909 and 1910 on an adjoining lot just west of the site of Lakeview Elementary. The largely undeveloped land that surrounded the site of the original building was owned by Collinwood resident Wallace Upton, one of the first rescuers on the scene. In an act of extraordinary generosity, he donated the land adjacent to the original site for the new building. In honor of his gesture, the grateful community named a street after him close to the new school.

Designed by architect Frank Barum, the new structure incorporated the safety features that the original building had so sorely lacked. Given the contemporary state of design and building materials, the school was as fireproof as possible, and each classroom had been outfitted with its own fire exit. The building was enlarged in 1917. The Cleveland School Board closed Memorial and three other Collinwood schools in 1979 due, in part, to population shifts and the declining number of school-age children in the area.

The building stood abandoned for more than two decades. Neighbors began reporting that at night a light would mysteriously appear in one of the now-vacant rooms and move slowly down the hallway, only to reverse direction and return to its point of origin. Police investigated but found nothing. Neighborhood children, especially teenagers in search of spooky adventure, entered the building at night and explored its dark hallways and musty classrooms. Since the abandoned school stood on the lot adjacent to the plot once occupied by Lakeview Elementary School, the notion that empty Memorial School was haunted quickly took hold.

The intrepid explorers who made these nocturnal forays reported that it seemed as if teachers and staff had simply abandoned the building on the spur of the moment, leaving everything behind. Chalk still lay in the trays below the blackboards; books, now covered with dust, were still stacked on the teachers' desks. In 2004, the derelict structure was finally demolished and replaced with a new Memorial School, which opened its doors in 2008.

· · ·

On Friday, March 7, 1908, the *Plain Dealer* reported that School Director Orr had suggested a monument be erected in "memory of the little folk of North Collinwood school who perished in the flames." Fittingly, the project would be paid for with donations from Cleveland's schoolchildren. Thus, on the evening of Sunday, March 9, the citizens of Collinwood gathered at the offices of the board of trade for a special meeting, at which it was decided that an organization should be created for the sole purpose of raising money for a memorial. This tribute to the victims of the fire would be placed in Lake View Cemetery on the spot where the nineteen unidentified children were buried. Hence, the organizers of the Collinwood School Children's Memorial Fund optimistically formulated plans to raise the needed funds from every school system in the state. Though by March 9 the organization boasted a total of $866 from Cleveland schoolchildren, funds did not pour in from outside the city. As the *Plain Dealer* had predicted on March 6, "It is easy to forget." It would be another two and a half years before the finished memorial, designed by sculptor Herman N. Matzen and installed by architect Frederic Steibinger, was unveiled in section 25 of Lake View Cemetery, on October 23, 1910.

In 1909, the Ohio General Assembly passed a bill mandating that "a memorial should stand in perpetuity to honor those who lost their

Herman N. Matzen's memorial to the victims of the fire stands in section 25 of Lake View Cemetery where the 19 unidenfied children are buried. (Photo by Mark Wade Stone. Courtesy StoryWorks.TV)

Louise Klein Miller's expansive memorial garden marked the site of the fire from 1918 through 1991. (Courtesy The Cleveland *Press* Collection, Michael Schwartz Library, Cleveland State University)

lives in this school fire tragedy." Apparently, in 1910, around the time of Collinwood's annexation to the city, the State of Ohio bought the land in question and deeded it the Cleveland Metropolitan School Board. Hence, Louise Klein Miller, curator of School Gardens and Grounds for the Cleveland Public School System, began working on plans for a memorial garden to be planted where Lakeview Elementary School originally stood. Actual work on the project, however, did not start until 1916 and was not completed until 1918. The resulting memorial was typical of the time: an overly extravagant Victorian affair, incorporating a touch of Versailles. The sprawling garden was 140 wide and 500 feet long. A fish pond, 30 by 50 feet, complete with a fountain, lily pads, and koi occupied the spot where most of the pupils had died. Although ultimate responsibility for the garden's upkeep rested with the school board, the pupils at the new Memorial School became its unofficial custodians. The garden included a greenhouse in which students grew and tended flowers to be placed in the memorial garden.

NOTES

The *General Slocum* was a sidewheel passenger ship that caught fire and burned in New York's East River on June 15, 1904, killing over one thousand people, primarily women and children from St. Mark's Evangelical Lutheran Church. The December 30, 1903, Iroquois Theater fire in Chicago killed at least six hundred people, thus becoming the worst single-building fire in American history.

Sarah Crosswy covers the development history of the crash bar in a 2016 blog entry for the International Museum of American History website.

EPILOGUE

DECLINE AND RENEWAL

There was no rest for the students who had survived the fire at Lakeview Elementary School. Still wrestling with the trauma of the disaster and the emotionally overwhelming weekend of funerals, the survivors returned to the classroom. Available stores and storage areas in the commercial sections of the village were commandeered for educational purposes and outfitted with desks and other school necessities. Although there is no existing record of how the surviving children and their parents felt about this rather insensitive attempt to return to "normal," classes resumed perhaps as early as Monday, March 9.

With the funerals and the public outrage over, stories concerning school safety slowly faded from Cleveland newspapers, leaving Collinwood to grieve alone. How does a community cope with the loss of so many children in a single catastrophic event? There is no well-trodden path marked with recognizable signposts that leads to anything like acceptance or understanding under such terrible circumstances. Any child born after 1900 who died in the fire would never even have been counted in the national census.

As time went on, the terrible tragedy faded from the region's consciousness, leaving Collinwood to mourn on its own and in silence. But events in the outside world occasionally offered the devastated community at least a few glimmering lights to ease it along the road to recovery. On October 2, 1908, Cleveland Naps pitcher Adrian "Addie" Joss pitched the fourth recorded perfect game in Major League Baseball history, and only the second in the American League, against the Chicago White Sox at League Park—giving the entire city, and especially its grieving neighbor to the east, something of which to be proud.

Euclid Beach Park had been a popular entertainment fixture along the Erie shore on the northwest edge of Collinwood since 1895. Conceived initially as an amusement park modeled after New York's Coney Island, Euclid Beach offered vaudeville acts, sideshows, a beer garden, gambling, and dancing. In 1909, the park got its first roller coaster, a John A. Miller New Velvet Coaster. In 1910, the original carousel was replaced by a Philadelphia Toboggan Company Carousel Number 19, an impressive affair containing fifty-eight horses and two Greek-style chariots. It remains unclear whether these additions were anything other than elements in normal park expansion, but coming when they did, the new rides offered the grieving community some needed diversion on its road to healing.

On January 21, 1910, the civic forces in Collinwood that had been lobbying for annexation with Cleveland finally won out. The tragedy at Lakeview Elementary School had focused a sharp light on the village's inabilities to provide adequate public services to its residents: a totally inadequate volunteer fire department, undermanned and poorly equipped, and a small police force, totally unable to control the massive crowds that flooded the village—congregating around the doomed building, clogging the streets, and intruding on the privacy of the grieving parents at the temporary morgue. The annexation finally eased those financial burdens with which the village had been struggling due to the rapid growth of the railroads and the explosion of its population.

· · ·

During World War II, Collinwood ranked as one of the largest and most compact industrial areas in the world. The intersection of East 152nd Street, St. Clair Avenue, and Ivanhoe Road—known as Five Points—became the commercial center of the neighborhood, and property values soared to levels held only by the most prestigious areas in the city proper. But one by one, the major industries began to depart, leaving behind an economically depressed area marked by empty storefronts, declining property values, and a host of social problems. In 1981, Conrail delivered what may have been the final economic blow to the struggling neighborhood when it closed the expansive railroad yards that had been among Collinwood's major employers since 1874.

Like so many older inner-city neighborhoods, Collinwood had to endure the crucible of blight and decay on its way to recovery. Beginning in the mid-1960s, serious racial violence erupted in Cleveland and added to Collinwood's list of woes. The Hough riots of 1966 and the far more serious Glenville shootout of 1968 rocked the city to its core. African American families began moving from violence-ravaged Glenville into the western section of Collinwood. On Tuesday, June 2, 1969, a mob of angry white students loitered around the high school after classes and began throwing rocks and bricks at passing cars containing black passengers. On June 4, police arrested eleven individuals, after a series of fistfights, beatings, and vandalism.

The seething racial tensions finally exploded on April 6, 1970, when more than three hundred white Collinwood High School students gathered outside the building and began pelting it with rocks, breaking more than fifty windows. Teachers hustled the two hundred black students into the school's third-floor cafeteria for protection. When the white mob moved into the building and began a rampage on the second floor, the black students began breaking the legs off of chairs to use as clubs. Teachers and officers from the Cleveland Police Department finally managed to restore at least some sense of order, and the black students were escorted out of the building, past the angry, jeering white students, into waiting buses to take them home. The violent episode prompted Cleveland mayor Carl Stokes to protect the school with a contingent of city police backed by the Ohio National Guard. But the racial clashes continued. In the fall of 1974, three black students were stabbed and a fourth was fatally shot.

During the 1970s, gang activity further blighted the declining neighborhood. The onetime altar boy turned gangster Daniel John Patrick Greene, better known as Danny Greene, moved back into Collinwood, the neighborhood into which he had been born, after having been booted out of St. Ignatius, a prestigious Catholic Jesuit high school in Ohio City on Cleveland's near west side. (Some sources allege he simply dropped out!) Back in the neighborhood, he formed his own criminal gang, the Celtic Club, and embarked on a career that combined legal land speculation with illegal loan-sharking and gambling.

During Greene's years at St. Ignatius High School, he had reportedly developed what would become a lifelong hatred of Italians. These hostilities and his greed led to a major conflict with the Cleveland branch of the Mafia. His ethnic prejudices, however, did not stop him from forming an alliance with local racketeer John Nardi, who harbored his own resentments against the local mob. The open warfare this struggle for dominance provoked resulted in so many bombings that Cleveland earned the title "Bomb City, USA." Greene became the Godfather of Collinwood, passing out money to the neighborhood's needy families, supporting local charities, and confronting the Hell's Angels when the motorcycle gang tried moving into the area. Though he escaped a bombing attempt at his Waterloo Road residence in 1975, he was killed in a car bomb explosion on October 6, 1977, after a visit to his Lyndhurst dentist.

. . .

The expansive memorial garden built on the site of Lakeview Elementary School between 1916 and 1918 became an unfortunate casualty of the neighborhood turmoil and decay, especially after 1979, when the Cleveland Board of Education closed Memorial School, which had been built on the adjacent lot to the west. With no one to care for it, the garden simply became an unattractive, wild field. In 1991, the Waterloo Business Association, in conjunction with local residents, built and planted a new garden—the scale less grand than its predecessor, but still a lovely, fitting memorial to those who lost their lives on that terrible day in 1908.

To preserve neighborhood history, the Collinwood Nottingham Historical Society was formed on February 19, 2009, just after the centennial of the tragic event. By April 2017, the memorial garden

The new memorial garden on the site of the fire, designed and landscaped in 1991. (Courtesy of the Collinwood Nottingham Historical Society)

had fallen victim to neglect, prompting Mary Louise Jesek Daley to declare in the *Collinwood Observer,* "It's a mess. We don't mean to demean it, but it is ceasing to be a meaningful memorial. The Garden itself is looking rather rough right now—and it deserves better." Thus, Collinwood residents Elva Brodnick and Charlotte Iafeliece spearheaded a campaign dubbed "The Little Red Cap Project," dedicated to cleaning up the site, replanting where necessary, and maintaining the twenty-five-year-old garden. In an act of homage, the Little Red Cap Project took its name from the story of Charlotte Iafeliece's uncle, John Pazicky, who died in the fire at the age of seven when he rushed back into the building to retrieve his red cap. Today, the organization is known as the Collinwood Fire Memorial Garden Project.

. . .

As the second decade of the twenty-first century comes to a close, Collinwood has become one of Cleveland's hot spots—a prime example of what today is affectionately termed "Rust Belt chic." In the 1990s, the neighborhood began its slow climb out of economic devastation and urban blight; as with many old city neighborhoods, the first signs of creeping revitalization arrived in the form of art galleries and small local restaurants, in the Waterloo Road area of North Collinwood. Arts Collinwood, established in 2003, was so successful in spearheading area redevelopment that the *Wall Street Journal* included the neighborhood in a 2009 story about fighting urban blight with art. With the support of a number of organizations, including the Greater Collinwood Development Corporation, the historic neighborhood continues to thrive. As of this writing, Collinwood boasts a population of around thirty-four thousand.

THE PERSISTENCE OF MEMORY

We unfortunately know very little about the subsequent lives of the major figures touched by the country's worst school fire; history rarely remembers the ordinary people swept up in extraordinary events. Once daily press coverage of the terrible story ceased, these people faded into the obscurities and vagaries of public records. In the weeks following the fire, the Township of Collinwood began awarding Carnegie Medals for heroism to those who had distinguished themselves during those chaotic hours on March 4; fifth-grade teacher Laura Bodey and Wallace Upton were among the recipients. The seven surviving teachers went their separate ways. The trauma they suffered that day is beyond comprehension, and they were left to cope on their own with the devastating loss of two colleagues, almost half of the student body, and their lingering memories of the terrible sights, sounds, and smells.

In 1908, no one had the vaguest idea what PTSD was. If you had suffered a tragic event, you simply pulled yourself up by your bootstraps and got on with it. There were no counseling services or support groups to ease you into acceptance of a life-altering trauma. Two of the surviving teachers tried escaping into marriage. First-grade teacher Pearl P. Lynn married Elliott Ray in 1909 and moved to Port Huron, Michigan, in 1910; Lulu M. Rowley, the third-grade teacher, married Henry Richards in that same year.

Three of the surviving teachers died within little more than a decade, all three only in their mid- to late thirties: English-born Laura L. Bodey in Auglaize, Ohio, in 1920; Lulu M. Rowley in 1919; Pearl P. Lynn in 1917. Lynn had sustained serious burns to her back during the ordeal, but it is unknown whether her injuries played any role in her early death. Similarly, it remains impossible to know whether the effects of lingering trauma hastened the deaths of the other two women. Kindergarten teacher Ethel A. Rose seems to have disappeared without a trace in the years following the fire. Three of the women did remain in education. According to the 1939 Cleveland City Directory, Ruby Irwin was still teaching thirty years after the disaster; German-born Katherine Gollmar still held a teaching position in Cleveland as late as 1922.

Out of the nine women at the Lakeview School, history chose to remember sixth-grade teacher and school principal Anna R. Moran. When Collinwood was annexed to Cleveland in 1910, she continued to work in the city school system as both teacher and principal. At her retirement in 1928, she moved to Lake Worth, Florida, where she died in her mid-eighties in 1949. Newspapers marked the occasion of her passing with memorial pieces that recalled and paid tribute to her role in the events of 1908.

Although he had been cleared of any culpability in the fire, janitor Fritz Hirter endured his neighbors' finger-pointing and icy stares for years. He kept quietly to himself and continued working in the Cleveland school system as a custodian, at least until 1930. The Hirters remained at 447 Collamer well into the 1940s—long after Collinwood's 1910 annexation to Cleveland, when local officialdom changed the name of the street to the much more prosaic East 152nd. He died in 1958 in Burton, Ohio—outside of Cleveland—at the age of ninety-five.

The pupils who died in the fire have been memorialized in print, stone, bronze, and cyberspace. Today, any knowledge of or reference to those who survived the catastrophe resides only in the memories and stories of their descendants. The only surviving student whose name has come down to the present is Emma Neibert, the fourteen-year-old fifth grader who first spotted the smoke on a trip to the basement bathroom. The widely published photograph of her taken the day of the fire eloquently catches the distress plainly visible on her face. Six days after the disaster, she testified at the inquest, accompanied by her father, Julius. In 1910, at sixteen, she married Oscar Fidler, a twenty-six-year-old Pennsylvania native who worked on the railroads and boarded in the Neibert household. The couple left Collinwood and moved to Indiana, where son Gilbert was born, but around 1913 they returned to the old neighborhood, where they remained. Daughter LaVerne was born in 1915. Oscar died in 1962; Emma followed, at the age of eighty-one, in 1975. Before internment, she rested in the Zele Funeral Home on East 152nd, where so many of her classmates and friends had lain nearly seventy years before.

IN MEMORIAM

By Saturday morning, March 7, the final tally of the dead had been established: 172 students and 2 teachers; a rescuer would be added to the total later. It has taken over a century, however, to arrive at a reasonably accurate accounting of all the children who perished in the catastrophe—all surnames spelled correctly and with proper first names: a century-long effort to retrieve identities from the obscuring shadows of the past. Although the number of students in each classroom seems to have been known at the time, and contemporary newspaper stories refer to names being checked off a list as identifications were made at the temporary morgue, no master list—if one ever existed—has come down to the present. It remains impossible to know how rigorous or casual record-keeping was at the school. At the time of this writing, there are a number of lists available on memorial plaques, on the Internet, or in printed form. Most contain errors, and all but Mary Louise Jesek Daley's are incomplete: the memorial at Lake View Cemetery has only 162 names, while Marshall Everett's list contains just 156 entries. The available lists include

1) the names inscribed on the memorial monument at Lake View Cemetery placed and dedicated in 1910
2) the list in Marshall Everett's book (1908)
3) Edward Kern's list in *The Collinwood School Fire of 1908* (1993)
4) the list of those buried in East Cleveland Township Cemetery (according to the cemetery records)

5) the list of those buried at both the Euclid City Cemetery and St. Paul's Cemetery

6) the list from *In Loving Remembrance,* a memorial tribute that the history department of the Cleveland Public Library compiled for its centennial exhibit, combining the list from the Lake View monument with Everett's (2008)

7) the marble tablet, containing the names of fifty children lost, that hung in the sanctuary of the former Calvary Presbyterian Church on East 152nd Street (1908)

8) Cristen Maxwell's "Collinwood School Fire Victims" virtual cemetery on the *Find a Grave* website

9) Michael Newbury's website *The Collinwood Fire, 1908*

10) the list compiled by Mary Louise Jesek Daley and Elva Brodnick of the Collinwood Nottingham Historical Society in 2018 for the 110th anniversary of the fire.

The difficulties of arriving at an accurate accounting of the victims began with the contemporary newspaper coverage of the disaster. Many of the last names that appeared in print were, at best, approximate. Reporters simply wrote down what they thought they heard, either at the site of the fire or at a victim's home; and when the source of the surname given was a Central European or Italian speaker with limited or no skills in the English language, the potential for simple misspellings or more radical distortions was obviously immense. Surnames with spelling differences can be particularly difficult to resolve. Wellick, Willick, Wickert, Weichert: are these four separate individuals or only two or three—perhaps even just one? Some of the first names that appeared in the contemporary newspaper coverage are simply wrong. If a reporter missed a victim's first name, he apparently would sometimes supply an Anglicized one that sounded reasonable. For example, in one instance, "Alvin" Sprung appears as "Johnnie" Sprung.

Mistakes in spelling have also been perpetuated for over a century. Sometimes a simple spelling error may be an annoyance to a researcher but is of little historical consequence. For example, Emma Neibert, who first noticed the smoke, initially appears in the *Press* as Emma Neubert; in other sources, she becomes Anna Neibert. In the 1900 Federal Census, the family name appears as Nebert—a clear indication that census records contain their own errors. Sometimes, however, what seems a simple spelling mistake can matter, indeed. Emma Neibert lost two siblings in the fire: her nine-year-old brother, John, and twelve-year-old sister, Olga; but that family connection went unrecognized by many commentators for over a century primarily because John and Olga were listed among the victims as "Neubert."

For the 110th anniversary of the disaster, Mary Louise Jesek Daley and Elva Brodnick of the Collinwood Nottingham Historical Society worked to produce a list of the children killed that was as complete and accurate as possible; they consulted contemporary newspaper stories, coroner's reports, city directories, and Federal Census documents. Aided by her familiarity with Central European names, especially the proper spellings, Daley traced the variants of the surnames from the 1908 lists through all the subsequent accountings—purging duplications, correcting misspellings, and establishing proper first names. In some circumstances, establishing victims' given names was very difficult. A nickname or shortened variant of the first name can have extraordinary staying power. If the press originally identified a child by an alternative version of his or her given name, that version was likely to stick and be repeated over the years as the list of those killed in the fire was expanded and updated. In such cases, Daley relied on the name as it appeared on the child's headstone. In some instances, the verification of a child's actual first name could be surprising. Since the day of the fire, one of the nine-year-old victims has been consistently identified as "Floy" Bravo. Common sense would seem to dictate that Floy was an obvious mistake and that the child's actual given first name was most likely Flo or Florence, perhaps even Floyd. Yet "Floy" is, indeed, what Mary Louise found engraved on the young girl's tombstone. By researching the burial sites of all the known victims, Daley and Brodnick have also tried to establish exactly who the nineteen unidentified were. Theoretically, those names for which there is no known internment site would be the nineteen unidentified children buried at Lake View Cemetery. Their work is complicated on the one hand by incomplete historical records and on the other by the fact that parents who could not identify the bodies of their children at the temporary morgue were allowed to bury one of the unidentified, and there is no record of how many, if any, parents did so.

The Collinwood Nottingham Historical Society list is as complete as possible, as well as the most accurate currently available. Published here for the first time, it contains 172 names. Where known, the sites of internment and the ages of the children at the time of death have been added. Determining a child's age would seem a simple matter; but contemporary newspapers make mistakes, and any child born after 1900 does not appear in the Federal Census.

Ila Adams, age 10
Woodland Cemetery

Irene Apari, age unknown

Adelbert Baldwin, age 12
Calvary Cemetery

Lauretta Baldwin, age 14
Harvard Grove Cemetery

Glenn A. Barber, age 11
   Although he sustained severe
burns and injuries from jumping
out of a second-floor window,
Glenn Barber survived the fire.
He died, however, early Saturday
morning, March 7, in Glenville
Hospital, thus becoming the last
of the children to lose his life.

Clayton Bell, age 14
West Park Cemetery

George Bluhm, age 14
Lake View Cemetery

Floy Bravo, age 9
East Cleveland Township Cemetery

Amelia Hazel Burrows, age 11
Mary Alice Burrows, age 12
East Cleveland Township Cemetery

Emma Marie Buschman, age 11
Rose Sophie Buschman, age 9
Euclid Cemetery

Marguerite Caravona, age 12
   Neighbors reported they could
hear the anguished cries of Marguerite Caravona's mother when
she learned her only child had
died in the disaster.

Nellie Carlson, age 13
Lake View Cemetery

George Centner, age 12
Lester Centner, age 8
East Cleveland Township Cemetery

Dale Clark, age 8
   Dale Clark was identified through a pink-bordered handkerchief in which he had wrapped a green marble.

Florence Mae Clayton, age 8
Lake View Cemetery

Mildred T. Cunningham, age 12
Lake View Cemetery

Paul Curran, age 14

Irene Davis, age 14
   Irene was one of the first to be identified in the temporary morgue. Her younger sister recognized a piece of her skirt that had survived the fire.

Percy Benjamin Day, age 11
East Cleveland Township Cemetery

Gretchen Dorn, age 10
Woodland Cemetery
   Gretchen was the daughter of Frank J. Dorn, member of the school board and chairman of its building committee. He was among the first to arrive on the scene and rescued several children.

Marija Drescik, age 10
Matilda Drescik, age 9
St. Paul's Cemetery
   Marija Drescik was identified by an earring.

Katherine Duffy, age 13
Calvary Cemetery

Albert Eichelberger, age 6

Florence Lillian Ewald, age 9
East Cleveland Township Cemetery

Katherine Gassmeier, age 12

Emily Gerbic, age 9
Calvary Cemetery

Alma Gilbert, age 11
Woodland Cemetery

Anton Golab, age 13

Ruth Gordon, age 9

Albert Gould, age 11
Mayfield Cemetery
    Albert Gould's sister recognized her brother by his shoes and the remnants of his sweater.

Raymond Gould, age 11
Euclid Cemetery
    Albert Gould's cousin Raymond was identified by a shirt-cuff button.

Earla Grant, age 13

Nathalie Marie "Mary" Greeshauge, age 9
East Cleveland Township Cemetery

Dorothy Lillian Hart, age 9
Spring Grove Cemetery

Claude Harvey, age 10

Edna Hebeler, age 13
Lake View Cemetery

Helene "Lena" Hefferle,
age 13 or 14
St. Paul Lutheran Cemetery, Berea

Emma Hennicke, age unknown
Peter Hennicke, age 13

Allen Bartlett Hinsdale, age 10
His distraught mother had
been told he survived the fire;
hence, she wandered the streets,
looking for him for days.

Walter Hirter, age 10
Helena Hirter, age 13
Ida Hirter, age 8
Lake View Cemetery
Four of janitor Fritz Hirter's
children were in attendance on
March 4. Only daughter Ella sur-
vived the catastrophe. Though
son Walter initially escaped, he
returned to search for his sisters.

Wilfred Hook, age 8

Esther Hummel, age 13
East Cleveland Cemetery

Herbert Alexander Hunter,
age 7
Lake View Cemetery

Francis Intihar, age 9
St. Paul's Cemetery

Emma Janke, age 7
Woodland Cemetery

Edward Kanowski, age 12
East Cleveland Township Cemetery

Fannie Kapudjija, age 9
Mary Kapudjija, age 11
St. Paul's Cemetery

Edward Kehl, age 10
Euclid Cemetery

Richard Dewey Kelley, age 10
Walter C. Kelley Jr., age 7
St. Johns Cemetery
　　Though newspaperman Walter
C. Kelley managed to identify the
body of his son Walter Jr., he was
initially unable to find and iden-
tify the body of his older son.

Anna Kern, age 9
St. Paul's Cemetery

Rudolph Kern Jr., age 12
Karolina Kern, age 10
St. Paul's Cemetery
　　The three Kern children
belonged to the extended family
of Edward Kern, author of *The
Collinwood School Fire of 1908*.
March 3 had been Rudolph Kern's
birthday; his grandfather had
given him a nickel as a present.
According to Edward, the boy was
identified by the coin, which had
melted onto the skin of his leg.

John Klisuric, age 14
St. Paul's Cemetery

Henry Kujat, age 13
Lake View Cemetery

Elizabeth "Lizzie" Lange, age 14
Lake View Cemetery

Ferdinand Leibritzer, age 9
Lake View Cemetery

Herbert Leonard, age 11
Arline K. Leonard, age 10
Louise Leonard, age 8
Lake View Cemetery

The grave marker for the three Leonard children lies close to the Collinwood School Fire victims' memorial in Lakeview Cemetery.

Harry Hutchinson Lodge, age 11
Lake View Cemetery

Twins **Clara** and **Florence Lowry**, ages 13
Lake View Cemetery

Josephine Mahlic, age unknown
St. Paul's Cemetery

Mary Marea, age unknown

Catharina Marinsek, age 7
St. Paul's Cemetery

Elmer Markuschatt, age 13
Elise Markuschatt, age 11
Lake View Cemetery

Otto Markuschatt fought with H. Zingleman over the identification of the body identified as Elmer Markuschatt. He also fought with Harry Sigler over the identification of the girl's body. Markuschatt won his claim of the male corpse, while Sigler maintained custody of the female body.

Hughie McIlrath, age 14
Highland Cemetery
    Hughie McIlrath was the son of
Charles McIlrath, chief of the Collinwood Police Department. After
identifying the body of his son at
the temporary morgue, McIlrath
returned to the scene of the fire
and stood guard into the night.

Edward Meirt, age 7
East Cleveland Township Cemetery

Tracy Miller, age 11

Gladys Mills, age 12

Jerca "Marie" Morelja, age 8
St. Paul's Cemetery
    Her parents identified her from
a small piece of fabric of her dress.

Lydia "Leda" Murphy, age 10

Rosa Nagel, age 13

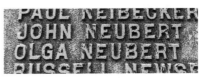

John Neibert, age 10
Olga Neibert, age 12
    John and Olga Neibert, as their
names appear on the memorial at
Lake View Cemetery. For over a
century, the misspelling of the last
name obscured the fact that they
were Emma Neibert's siblings.
The mistake wasn't caught until I
checked census records in 2018.

Paul Neubecker, age 7

Russel Newsberry, age 13
    John Newsberry identified his
son through a small watch chain.

John Oblak, age 13
St. Paul's Cemetery
    John Oblak's mother recognized her son from a piece of
clothing.

Joseph Opalek, age 11
Josephine Opalek, age 12
Calvary Cemetery

Edna May Pahner, age 13

Harry Parr, age 8
Lake View Cemetery
    Harry Parr had been home for
three weeks with a broken arm.
March 4 was his first day back at
school. Edward Kern relates that
William J. Parr identified his son
through a fragment of under-
clothing.

Frederick Paul, age 13
Ruth Marie Paul, age 7
Lake View Cemetery

John Pazicky, age 7
St. Mary's Cemetery

John Pazicky initially escaped
the inferno, but he lost his life
when he ran back in the building
to retrieve his new red cap.

Frank Perat, age 9
Mary Perat, age 11
St. Paul's Cemetery

Emma Jane "Jennie" Phillis,
age 14
Lake View Cemetery
    Jennie's mother managed to
reach the west exit but could not
pull her from the pile of tightly
packed children plugging the doorway. She stayed with her daughter,
holding her hand and brushing
the flames away from her hair until
she was driven back by the heat
and a piece of falling glass. At the
temporary morgue, she identified
her daughter afrom a ring she had
received as a Christmas present.

Victor Polomsky, age 9
Calvary Cemetery
    John Polomsky identified his
son by a small bit of cloth that
clung to the boy's arm. The material
matched that of his mother's apron.

John Popovic, age 13
Calvary Cemetery

Gretchen Puppel, age 7
East Cleveland Township Cemetery

Louis Quirk, age 12

Harvey Reeves, age 9
St. Paul's Cemetery

Adam Rehan, age 12

Mary Ridgeway, age 8

Clara Ritzi, age 10
Helen Ritzi, age 8

Fern Robinson, age 9
Wanita Robinson, age 7
Euclid Cemetery
    The Robinson sisters were the only students of color at the school. Their race was never specified in the contemporary news coverage.

John Rochinsky, age unknown

Lily Rommelfanger, age 9
St. Paul's Cemetery
    Lily was a cousin of the three Kern children killed in the fire.

Emil Otto Rostock, age 14
Lillian Carrie Rostock, age 6
Euclid Cemetery

Don Rush, age 13
Lake View Cemetery
    Wednesday, March 4, was Don Rush's birthday. His father identified his son through a small charm he had given him as a present.

Anthony Samsa, age 12
Mary Samsa, age 11
Rose Samsa, age 10
St. Paul's Cemetery

Glen Sanderson, age 12

Harold Sanderson, age 9

George Schaffer, age 9
Riverside Cemetery
    Unable to extricate his son from the wedge of children at the west exit, W. C. Schaffer stood by the boy, holding his hand, and offering what comfort he could as the flames approached.

Emma Schmidt, age 10
Mildred "Dolly" Schmidt, age 10
Lake View Cemetery
    An angel monument with "Our Dolly" engraved on it marks the interment site. Emma's name appears on the side.

Willie Schmidt, age unknown

Edward Scholl, age 10

Verna Schubert, age 12

Henry E. Schultz, age 9
Lake View Cemetery
    Henry Schultz's distracted mother had gone from body to body looking for her son. Reportedly, she kept calling his name as she clawed at the fragments of clothing that adhered to each corpse. He was ultimately identified through the pattern of his sweater.

Mary Sega, age 11
Calvary Cemetery

Norman P. Shepherd, age 11
Lake View Cemetery

Morris C. Shepphard, age 14
East Cleveland Township Cemetery

Norris Ackroid Sherman, age 10
Harvard Grove Cemetery

Mabel Sigler, age 10
Lake View Cemetery

Gilbert Skelley, age 8
Madge Skelley, age 12

Pauline Skerl, age 13
Marcelline Avenue Cemetery

Fred Swanson, age 7
Hulda Swanson, age 13
Edward Swanson, age 12
Woodland Cemetery
    Hulda Swanson could only be identified by a recently filled tooth.

Willie Smith, age 9
East Cleveland Township Cemetery

Elizabeth Sodoma, age 12
Emma Sodoma, age 10
Julius Sodoma, age 8
Lake View Cemetery

William Eugen Southwell, age 12
Harvard Grove Cemetery

Alvin H. Sprung, age 7
East Cleveland Township Cemetery

Rosella Stewart, age 14

Nils Thompson, age 10
Thomas Thompson, age 7
Woodland Cemetery
    Nils Thompson was the first child to be identified. His widowed mother recognized a suspender buckle. Nils had initially escaped unharmed but returned to the burning building to find his younger brother.

Luella B. Walden, age 10
East Cleveland Township Cemetery
   At the beginning of the school
year, Luella's third-grade teacher,
Grace Fiske, had appointed her
"monitor of the fire drill," a position in which she took great pride.

Henry Weichert, age 11
Lake View Cemetery

James Turner, age 14
Maxwell Turner, age 6
Norman Turner, age 9
Oswego New York Cemetery, buried with their grandmother
   Their father had come to Collinwood to work on the Lake Shore &
Michigan South railroad. The family had resided in Collinwood for
only a few months. James Turner
managed to get out of the doomed
building, but he ran back to search
for his two younger siblings. All
three were killed in the fire.

Josephine Urbancic, age 7

Anna Vidmar, age 12
Sophia Vidmar, age 10
St. Mary's Cemetery

Eva Wachhaus, age 7
Ida Wachhaus, age 8
Woodland Cemetery

Willie Weisberg, age 10

Annie Wellick, age 11, holding a child we must assume is a younger sibling

Edgar Thomas Woodhouse, age 9
Lake View Cemetery
    Edgar Woodhouse was one of the final two victims to be positively identified, on the morning of Monday, March 9—the day the nineteen unidentified were buried at Lake View Cemetery.

William Worthington Wells, age 12
Calvary Cemetery

Clara H. A. Wendorff, age 12
Woodland Cemetery

Robert "Robbie" Wickert, age 10
Woodland Cemetery

Annie Woodhouse, age 12

Arnold Woodrich, age 7
Meta Woodrich, age 11
Woodland Cemetery

John Zimmerman, age 8
Louise Zimmerman, age 13
Calvary Cemetery

Harry R. Zingelman, age 8
Lucy E. Zingelman, age 10
Lake View Cemetery

Mary Zitnik, age unknown

Angela Zupan, age 11?
Marguerite Zupan, age 11
St. Paul's Cemetery

NOTES

The ages that appear here have been culled from Edward Kern's *The Collinwood School Fire of 1908* and Cristen Maxwell's virtual cemetery "The Victims of the Collinwood School Fire." Mary Louise Jesek Daley supplied the internment sites.

All the portraits of the children who died in the fire pictured here originally appeared in Marshall Everett's *Complete Story of the Collinwood School Disaster and How Such Horrors Can Be Prevented*. Obviously some of these photographs predate—sometimes by years—the fire.

The photos of the grave markers are by Mark Wade Stone, courtesy StoryWorks. TV.

BIBLIOGRAPHY

BOOKS

Annals of the Early Settlers Association of Cuyahoga County. Cleveland: Mount
& Carroll, 1880.

Bellamy, John Stark. *Cleveland's Greatest Disasters.* Cleveland: Gray, 2009.

Coates, William. *A History of Cuyahoga County and the City of Cleveland.* Chicago:
American Historical Society, 1924.

Everett, Marshall. *Complete Story of the Collinwood School Disaster and How Such
Horrors Can Be Prevented.* Cleveland: N. G. Hamilton, 1908.

Kern, Edward. *The Collinwood School Fire of 1908.* Cleveland: E. Kern, 1993.

Taylor, Troy, and Rene Kruse. *And Hell Followed with It.* Alton, IL: Whitechapel
Productions Press, 2010.

Van Tassel, David D., and John J. Grabowski, eds. *The Encyclopedia of Cleveland
History.* Bloomington: Indiana University Press, 1987.

[Weiler, Gustav.] *In Memoriam: Katherine C. Weiler.* Pittsburgh: Pittsburgh Print-
ing Co., 1908.

DOCUMENTS AND ARCHIVAL SOURCES

Cleveland Inspection Bureau. "Editorial Comment and Report of the Collinwood School Disaster." Cleveland, Apr. 6, 1908. Collinwood School
Fire Centennial: Documents and News Articles. Cleveland Public Library.

Cuyahoga County, Office of the Medical Examiner. Documents relating to
the Death of Katherine Weiler, et al., case no. 11325. Cuyahoga County
Office of the Medical Examiner, Cleveland.

Fallon, Michael F. "Firsthand Report of the Collinwood School Fire." Cleveland, 1908. Collinwood School Fire Centennial: Documents and News Articles. Cleveland Public Library.

Village of Collinwood. "Council Proceedings." Mar. 1908. Collinwood School Fire Centennial: Documents and News Articles. Cleveland Public Library.

Visiting Nurses Association. "Minutes of Board Meeting." Apr. 1, 1908.

JOURNAL ARTICLES

"Fatal Fire in a Cleveland School: Great Loss of Life Caused by Poor Fire Escape Regulations." *Fire and Water Engineering* (Jan. 1, 1908): 160.

Grant, Casey C. "Collinwood's Hardest Lesson: The Lake View School Fire." *National Fire Protection Association Quarterly* 102, no. 5 (2008): 64–72.

"Major School Disasters: Lakeview School, Collinwood, Ohio, March 4, 1908." *Quarterly of the National Fire Protection Association* (Oct. 1939): 162–64.

NEWSPAPER ARTICLES

Burke, Thomas A. "Where Was Janitor? Is Burke's Inquiry." *Cleveland Press,* Mar. 7. 1908, 1.

Dale, Dorothy. "Fathers and Mothers Weep for Little Ones in O'er a Hundred Homes," *Cleveland Press,* Mar. [6?] 1908.

——. "Teachers Are Fire Heroines." *Cleveland Press,* Mar. 5, 1908.

DeMarco, Laura. "Horrific Collinwood School Fire of 1908 Remembered in New Movie." *Cleveland Plain Dealer,* Oct. 27, 2016.

Guenther, Wally. "The Collinwood Fire: A Survivor Recalls the Tragedy of 70 Years Ago When 174 Died." *Cleveland Plain Dealer,* Mar. 19, 1978.

Hamilton, Barbara J. "100th Anniversary of the Collinwood School Disaster." *Gazette* (Jefferson, OH), Mar. 26, 2008.

Lothman. Daniel. "The Collinwood School Disaster." *Cleveland Plain Dealer,* Mar. 4, 1933.

McGunagle, Fred. "Our Century 1908: Horror in Collinwood: 172 Students Die in City's Worst Disaster." *Plain Dealer,* Mar. 29, 1998.

Rowley, Lulu. "Pupils Fled Like Sheep into Trap, Says Teacher." *Cleveland Press,* Mar. 6, 1908.

Silverman, Alvin. "Explodes 'Myth' on '08 Collinwood Fire." *Cleveland Plain Dealer,* 1938.

Spindle, Peg. "Don't Sell This Land, Sob Grief-Stricken Moms." *Cleveland News,* Mar. 4, 1965.

Wallace, George A. "Partitions at Sides of Rear Doors of School Were Jaws of Death Trap." *Cleveland Press,* Mar. 6, 1908, 1.

Wooley, Edna K. "Morbid Vultures Prey Upon Grief." *Cleveland News,* Mar. 6, 1908.

Zatik, Louise. "'Cutting of the Flowers' Will Honor 1908 Collinwood School Fire Victims." *Sun News* (Cleveland), Mar. 27, 2008.

INTERNET SOURCES

Bullock, William Hubern. *Collinwood School Fire: March 4, 1908* (film). Posted by the Cleveland Public Library. Feb. 16, 2008, https://www.youtube.com/watch?v=-KQU-DR9z2c).

Cleveland Public Library Department of Fine Arts. "Rare Film of 1908 Collinwood School Fire." *Regional Economics Action Links North East Ohio.* Feb. 28, 2008, http://realneo.us/news/2008/02/28/rare-film-of-1908-collinwood-school-fire.

Cooke, Judy. *Iroquois Theater: Website Devoted to 1903 Iroquois Theater Fire in Chicago.* 2019, http://www.iroquoistheater.com/.

Crosswy, Sarah. "The Collinwood School Disaster Influenced Fire Safety Protocols." *O Say Can You See: Stories from the Museum.* International Museum of American History website. Oct. 14, 2016, https://americanhistory.si.edu/blog/collinwood-disaster-fire-safety.

DeMarco, Laura. "Horrific Collinwood School Fire Remembered in New Movie." *Cleveland.com.* Oct. 27, 2016, https://www.cleveland.com/entertainment/2016/10/horrific_collinwood_school_fir.html.

Fearing, Heidi. "Collinwood High School Riots." *Cleveland Historical.* Last updated Oct. 13, 2017, https://clevelandhistorical.org/items/show/392.

Macdonald, Jim. "Ash Wednesday." *Making Light* (blog). Mar. 4, 2011, https://nielsenhayden.com/makinglight/archives/012875.html.

Martens, Benno. "A Walk through North Collinwood." *Belt Magazine.* Feb. 24, 2016. https://beltmag.com/a-walk-through-north-collinwood/.

Maxwell, Cristen. "Collinwood School Fire Victims: A Virtual Cemetery,"

Find a Grave. Accessed Oct. 10, 2018, https://www.findagrave.com/virtual
-cemetery/21145.

Namsick, J. R. *Collinwood School Fire Repository.* 2019, http://www.collinwood
fire.com/.

Newbury, Michael. *The Collinwood Fire, 1908.* Accessed Sept. 28, 2018, https://
collinwoodfire.org/.

Ockerbloom, John Mark, ed. "Online Books by Marshall Everett." *The Online
Books Page.* Accessed June 7, 2019, https://onlinebooks.library.upenn.edu
/webbin/book/search?author=Everett%2C+Marshall&amode=words.

Taylor, Troy. "I Had to Leave My Little Child to Die: Horrors and Hauntings
of the Collinwood School Fire." *American Hauntings.* Mar. 4, 2013, https://
www.americanhauntingsink.com/collinwood.

INDEX